MY
HIDDEN
RACE

MY
HIDDEN
RACE

ANYIKA ONUORA

MIRROR BOOKS

To Dad, Dalu ezigbo nnam na ngozi
na nkwado gi nine maka odi nmam.
Chukwu gozie

MIRROR BOOKS

Published in Great Britain and Ireland in 2021 by
Mirror Books, a Reach PLC business,
5 St Paul's Square, Liverpool, L3 9SJ.

www.mirrorbooks.co.uk
@TheMirrorBooks

Hardback ISBN: 9781913406790
eBook ISBN: 9781913406806

Photographic acknowledgements:
Anyika Onuora, Alamy, Reach Plc.

Design and production by Mirror Books.
Edited by Chris Brereton and Simon Monk.
Additional proofing: Laura McConville.

Printed and bound by CPI Group (UK) Ltd,
Croydon, CR0 4YY.

Contents

Foreword:
Tony Bellew

I'VE SAID it many times before, Liverpool was a tough place to grow up. I was raised by a black mother and a white father.

When I went to the north end of the city, I was considered white, and then on the south end, I was considered black. I experienced a decent amount of under-the-radar racism, but it's nothing compared to what Anyika dealt with as a child.

Anyika grew up in the same area as my wife Rachael, and it's the sort of place where people know each other. Anyika's family are wonderful people, and they instilled in her the work ethic and determination that took her to the top of her sport.

Sadly, the Onuoras also had to deal with untold horrific racism on the streets they called home. They faced raw hatred that nobody should ever have to experience.

I first got to know Anyika through my training at the athletics track in Liverpool. I was there most Saturdays when preparing for fights, trying to get through 800 metres in three minutes.

I used to watch Anyika and the other world-class athletes from this city like Katarina Johnson-Thompson in a state of awe. I idolised their talent on the track. People think that athletics is a God-given talent, but I saw what Anyika put into this sport, and her achievements were founded on brutally hard work day after day.

Liverpool is a city that will always support its own. I am a massively passionate Everton supporter, and Anyika is a lifelong Liverpool fan, but that will never matter, we were tightly bound as Scousers.

I would always try to watch her compete all over the world, and I would regularly check her results. I was lucky enough to feel the love and support of this city when I fought, and it was exactly the same when Anyika ran. Her Olympic bronze in Rio was proof of what is possible, no matter where you come from in Liverpool, you can achieve your dreams.

I am passionate that young girls need positive role models, and I can't think of a better one than Anyika. She was a world-class athlete with Olympic, Commonwealth and World Championship medals, who also was determined to reach the highest level academically.

In Liverpool, we have young girls who can feel hopeless about their future, they grow up in a tough environment and can't see any way through. I want them to look at Anyika as an example that it doesn't matter the challenges that are laid before you, with tenacity and grit, you can get anywhere you want, and win at the highest level.

Anyika went through a hell of a lot more than I can ever imagine. As a young black girl in this city, she dealt with prejudice and discrimination that was vicious. Through a strong foundation of love from her family, she grew up determined to make her mark in life and she certainly did. Anyika was never just going to be an ordinary student at school, and she was never just going to be an ordinary athlete.

For any young girl who needs an example of what is possible, I will point them to Anyika. She always had an absolute refusal to accept the status quo, and instead drove herself to be a world-class athlete and a leader in her community.

I am proud to know Anyika, and I know that Liverpool is equally as proud of everything that she has achieved and will continue to achieve for years to come.

Tony Bellew, April 2022

Prologue:
The Time Is Now

I HAVE sat in athletics call rooms all over the world, some big, some small, all of them featureless.

They are the places that you go just before you step onto the track to compete, a purgatory for athletes. They vary in size and shape, but I hate almost every single one of them.

Athletics has chewed me up and has not even had the decency to spit me out properly.

I have seen and experienced things as a British athlete that haunt me during the day and the night. No matter how hard I try, I will never be able to outrun the demons in my mind.

I have been brutally sexually assaulted, experienced frequent racial abuse and have attempted suicide twice. All of this happened while I was competing for my country.

I used to believe in the sanctity of the Olympic spirit, watching my heroes on the telly with my Dad; but not now.

The individual dreams and hopes of the athlete don't matter; they are ultimately a means to an end.

You are a lycra-clad cog in a machine that is designed to churn out more metal at the podium, which will hopefully generate a sustainable financial model for UK Athletics for many years to come. I am now in the most critical call room of my life, just before the final of the women's 4x400 metres at the 2016 Rio Olympics. As usual, once I enter this room, I feel absolutely alone. My teammates are just beside me, but they might as well be in another country.

I am silently urging the clock's hands to move that bit quicker, to release me from this holding pen and to accept my fate on the track, but it's hopeless. I know the thin margins of errors that exist in my sport.

You must emerge from this room, walk into a crowded stadium and run the best race of your life. If only it was that simple.

I hear the words of the senior UK Athletics figure ringing in my ear.

"I hope these girls are fucking ready," they say. "There's 10 million quid in funding on the line if they don't get a medal. I'm telling you, they better fucking get this together tonight."

I wasn't meant to hear these words. I heard them as I was in the team huddle before we went out onto the track and they have successfully turned my anxiety levels up a notch.

The official talked about us as if we are an unpredictable index fund on the London Stock Exchange, not four women who have sacrificed everything to be at the Olympics.

I shouldn't be surprised. And after over a decade with UK Athletics, I'm not.

I try to crowd these thoughts out of my head and look

around the room at my teammates. They are calm on the surface, and that at least tricks me into focusing on the job at hand. Finally, and mercifully, we are told that it is time to race and leave the room in single file.

I have a final chance to win an Olympic medal, and despite this sport having savagely broken me mentally and physically, assaulting my body and mind, I am ready to run my perfect race.

The personalities of the athletes you race against are always interesting. Are you competing against the Jamaicans and the Americans? They are almost certainly going to be loud and hyped up. They can psyche you out before you've even stepped onto the starting blocks if you let them.

The Eastern Europeans and the Scandinavians, conversely, are generally cold and calm, not even slightly affected by distractions before the race. Then, most difficult of all, there are athletes from different countries who will cheerfully chat to you as if you are in the doctor's waiting room idly leafing through a celebrity gossip magazine, not about to go to war on the track.

I am one of the leaders in this 4x400 team and feel a level of responsibility to protect and mentor the younger athletes, not just on the track, but off it. The 400 metres combines the strategy of a chess grandmaster with the explosive cardiovascular needs of a sprinter. It combines brain with brawn, and at its best is an incredible spectacle.

We have a whole track to complete at almost full speed

and our hopes, dreams and bank accounts are built on each precise footstep of the rubber surface. We know our breathing patterns so well that our bodies have almost become a finely tuned vehicle that we must drive to its maximum capabilities before it burns out completely.

I can hear the roar of the crowd and breathe in slowly and deeply using my diaphragm to quell the surging tension in my body. At times like this, I usually find solace in prayer, but there is just too much adrenaline flowing. My mind starts to play tricks on me, asking me questions that I do not want to answer.

'What happens if you trip up? Maybe you might pull your hamstring, I know it's been feeling a bit tight. No? You're totally sure? I reckon it's ready to pop! Ok, Anyika, no, I've got it girl. Let's go with the old classic, what the hell are you going to do if you drop that slippery baton in front of hundreds of millions of people? You'll look a state on YouTube for years to come. Kids will be laughing in every playground in the country at you. Just imagine that.'

This is a game that my mind plays on me at the very worst of times and I am never a willing participant. I allow myself to look around the stadium and see the comforting sight of British flags in the stands.

Far from home, I know that there are people here willing us to win a medal and upset the odds. We face the might of the Americans and the world champion Jamaican team, but on our day, I know we are capable of anything.

Prologue

I stand at the side of the track and plot out the course mentally, where I need to accelerate, and where I need to ensure that I don't burn all of my energy and get crippled completely by lactic acid. Running second in the team, I will have to maintain our position, or worse, claw it back if needs be. If I have a bad race, our fragile house of cards will fall. A lifetime of preparation and sacrifice for this moment and my part of this race will be over in a little over 50 seconds if everything goes to plan.

I hear the starting gun and it snaps me out of my swirling mental fog. I will stand ready, counting down the seconds until I move off my mark ready to receive the baton.

After the life that I have lived, I know that this race will be something to savour. I have had to teach myself how to walk again and to trust a world that so often has violently dragged me face down through the dirt.

My mind is finally calloused and my body hardened for a race that I will never forget as long as I live.

The time is now, and I cannot let my people down.

1

Life Lessons

FROM A young age, I was taught that life wasn't fair.

My parents, Nkoli and Chiz, arrived in Britain as immigrants from Nigeria and passed on a brutal – but important – message to me. I was told that as a young black girl, I could never be satisfied with being merely good; I had to be the best at everything I did.

For years, my parents had dealt with racism, whether subtly or directly, and they knew that as a black person in Britain you had to fight hard to change someone's immediate conscious or subconscious negative impression of you.

In West African culture, hard work is not a choice, it's a necessity. Families in Nigeria understand that if they do not take the right opportunities at school, they might miss out on jobs that can provide for their extended family. If they do not work hard at their job, they know that there is no safety net for them if they lose it. Across the world, if you ask anyone with Nigerian parents, they will share similar experiences. Graft is the rigid spine that holds our families together. Homework is not only done to a high standard every night, but extra revision is completed to ensure successful exam results. You have a paper round before you do your homework? Well kid, you better make damn sure that nobody has ever delivered the *Liverpool Echo* around the neighbourhood better than you.

The England rugby international Maro Itoje grew up in a Nigerian household and he once joked in an interview, "What's the best way to scare Nigerian parents? Tell them that you're going to focus on music as a career." I understand what he is saying perfectly. In most Nigerian families, there is a clearly laid path filled with hard work at school and university that hopefully will lead to a safe and secure career, be it as a teacher or an accountant, with extra points awarded at family gatherings if you become a lawyer or a doctor.

My life was a bit different. The sacrifices of my parents eventually provided me with the platform and opportunities to run on the greatest athletics tracks in the world. Without their love and support, I wouldn't be sitting down to write this book. I burst out of the starting blocks and took a different path to what they expected, but they were always proud to support me on and off the track.

In a way, seeing me wearing my Great Britain vest reminded them that their hard work and difficulties since arriving in this country had been worth it.

My father and mother are from Nri, Nigeria, an area that is understood to be the motherland and cradle of Igbo ethnicity. The Igbo people are renowned in Nigeria for their cultural traditions, family values and skill in commerce and farming.

My Dad grew up in a village governed by strict standards, where family and elders were put first, and individual needs or desires were only relevant if they were useful to the broader society.

The expectations of academic success that were placed on my father, and which would eventually fall on me, drove him to gain qualifications in accountancy and seek employment far from the sun-kissed land of his ancestral village that he knew and loved.

In the late fifties, Dad would move to the cold climate of Glasgow, Scotland, where he found work in the finance department of the city's docks, mercifully sheltered from the fierce and icy wind that frequently blew off the River Clyde.

Arriving in Glasgow with his first wife, Chiz Onuora was far from everything that he knew and loved. His home village in Nri was a place where generations of families socialised together, bonding over games of 'Ayo', a traditional Nigerian pursuit, where the seeds hit the six pits in the board with a satisfying thump.

In Glasgow, he and his young wife were often the only two black faces in a tough and uncompromising city where your bones never quite seemed to stay warm and dry for long.

My father knew that his primary focus, beyond looking after his wife and his eventual brood of children, was building his career at the docks. Dad never told me about racism that he experienced directly, but that doesn't mean to say that it didn't happen.

He always refused to let negative experiences define him, instead, he preferred to always look forwards.

Dad only looked for the good in people, and in Glasgow, he found solace in his work that kept him busy until well after the shipyard whistle went and the men rushed home to their dinners. My father could never be an ordinary accountant; he had to be the best bean counter that had ever worked by the side of the River Clyde.

He knew the lazy racist stereotypes that people would be quick to label him with as an African man, and he therefore ensured that his dedication and numerical talents quickly made him indispensable to his company.

Dad built a family in Glasgow, with children who would eventually become my half-siblings, but unfortunately, his migrant marriage in Scotland didn't work out. Once again, finding comfort in his career, Dad found work in another British dockside city with a familiar cool and damp climate.

Liverpool would become my father's adopted home for the rest of his adult life, punctuated by frequent long visits home to his ancestral village in Nigeria, where he eventually built a beautiful home for his family.

His marriage had ultimately broken up, and after two

years, during a holiday back home in Nri, he met my mother, Nkoli.

By the late 1960s, Dad had achieved some financial security as an accountant and had built lasting friendships in Liverpool, particularly at the city's Igbo Club in Toxteth, a cherished Nigerian social hub that would later become a large part of my life.

Dad was able to afford to return to Nigeria on yearly visits to visit relatives and bring long-awaited and prized gifts to the village that could only be sourced in the United Kingdom. He had left his home with sadness as a young man and was now able to return to his beloved homeland as a man who, in the eyes of the extended community, had made a successful life abroad as an accountant.

Although my Dad was mostly very happy in Liverpool, I believe that he truly came alive in his home village. In Nri he was always known as *nwata buluaku*, translated from Igbo as "child from the big family." This name was bestowed on him as the first son in a large and respected family that had deep roots all over his fertile homeland.

He would sit long into the night drinking palm wine with old friends and families that his people had known for generations. Lengthy stories about village families and ancestors were told long into the night in Igbo. People in the village were never forgotten as long as their stories were told by the fire.

Heritage was important to Dad, and he listened when one

of the village's female elders told him that she had a daughter who he should meet immediately. My father quickly agreed, not wanting to offend this respected elder, and that's how he met my mother.

My mother was beautiful then, and she still is to this day. Tall and elegant, you never forget meeting Nkoli Onuora. Dad certainly never did. I can understand why he was so attracted to that young woman, in her expertly tailored traditional dress that is common in Nigeria with her hair always perfectly styled in braids.

Mum had studied finance at university and her application and talent had led to her working on some of the earliest computer programming in Africa. After a brief courtship, Mum and Dad eventually married and returned to live in Liverpool, settling in the suburb of Wavertree, in the south of the city.

My early memories of Wavertree are all happy ones. I close my eyes, and I see my aunties in their traditional dresses fussing over the food on the stove, while mounds of jollof rice and steaming bowls of pepper soup are placed on the table for family and friends to enjoy.

Dad had eventually managed to buy his first house, but not without difficulty. Although there was a larger Nigerian community in Liverpool than in Glasgow, he and his friends were very much a minority in a sea of white faces going to work on the bus every day.

For months, nobody was willing to sell Chiz Onuora a

home in Liverpool until he finally got a break. Dad was only able to purchase his house in full, in cash, from a local Jewish man. There was no mortgage plan, or meetings with the friendly local bank manager, who might enjoy the business of a successful local accountant with an impeccable financial history.

Dad's professional success was irrelevant at that moment, and for many years after it. Contrary to his wishes, he was defined by the colour of his skin, not by his character, and he had to take any opportunity he could grab.

The house in Wavertree was not luxurious, but it was large and an endless place of fascination for me, my siblings and our neighbours. There was a large attic to play in, where we created our own version of C.S Lewis' Narnia, far from the adults downstairs, forgetting that we were in suburban Liverpool for a moment. There was a mix of cultures on our street and we were warmly welcomed by the local community and our neighbours.

I was born in 1984, in a season that Liverpool FC won the First Division and the European Cup, and I had little choice but to begin a lifelong devotion to the Reds. In games of street football as a young girl, I was Ian Rush scoring goals for fun in the Merseyside derby, drilling shots expertly through jumpers that served as goalposts, past the hapless neighbour's son who had to pretend to be the Everton's portly but skilled goalkeeper, Neville Southall. I knew from a young age that I was blessed with speed, but this was simply put down to youthful exuberance. I had a tremendous amount of energy to burn off and the streets of Wavertree became the perfect playground.

I was extremely close to my brother, Chiz Junior, who was two years older than me and a talented athlete in his own right and I quickly became his shadow on the streets of Wavertree. Chiz got my Mum's good looks and my Dad's easy charm.

He grew up tall and strong and would quickly establish himself as his sisters' protector on the streets of Liverpool. Whenever we needed him, he was always there. I was a good child, but he was constantly getting into trouble with his gang of mates on their bicycles. He was a loveable rogue, at the centre of any mischief, but almost always able to charm his way out of trouble.

We would regularly play hide and seek on the street and one day Chiz took his competitive edge too far, finding himself above a mechanic's roof. Unable to come down on his own, Chiz managed to fall off the roof, getting a large gash and bruises from falling directly onto a barbed wire wall.

A friend of the family eventually found him and he said that he'd just fallen in the street. Once he got to the hospital with Mum, the nurse became convinced that he was a victim of domestic violence as the injury looked far worse than a fall on the street.

It was only when the nurse spoke to Chiz in private that he confessed to his acrobatics across the roof on the condition that she wouldn't tell Mum. Chiz only revealed the truth to Mum recently, well into his thirties.

Although Chiz was never too far from mischief, it was his quick actions as a 10-year-old that saved my life. Chiz, my sister Nkechi and I had been invited to the local leisure centre in Wavertree for a friend's birthday. We were all excited at the prospect of a swimming pool with slides and as much birthday cake as we could eat.

We arrived at the pool, and Chiz didn't waste any time in doing a spectacular cannonball into the water to the approval of our young friends. Nkechi and I shuffled out of the changing rooms together and, gazing up at the slide that everyone was enjoying, we eventually decided to join them.

When we got to the top of the stairs, Nkechi insisted that I should go first as the eldest while I insisted that she should go first as the youngest so I was there to look after her. In the end, with a growing crowd behind us getting restless, we decided that I should go.

I went down the slide quickly, and just before I hit the water, I realised that I had made a huge mistake. I had thought that this slide would enter the shallow water, which was all I could handle being an extremely weak swimmer.

I hit the deep water, and in seconds, I was helpless and drowning. I felt the water enter my nose, and lungs, my body sinking to the pool floor quickly. I completely blacked out.

I eventually woke, coughing up chlorinated water on the cool surface of the pool deck, not sure what had happened.

It turned out that Chiz had seen me hit the water and had immediately dived in, dragged me out, and then, aged just 10 don't forget, he had started performing CPR, bringing me back to life just as the lifeguards arrived.

When I opened my eyes, Chiz was uncharacteristically frantic. "Are you ok? Anyika? You nearly drowned, me Mum is gonna kill ya!" I was too stunned to reply so just lay there like an exhausted frog. I was scared, but also embarrassed that the whole leisure centre was now looking at me. Chiz resumed control, "Right, we'll deal with this later." Casting off his brief moment of heroics, and maturity casually, Chiz performed a spectacular cannonball back into the pool and the party was back to normal.

It turned out that Chiz didn't have to deal with the drowning again. One of the parents at the pool had phoned my parents, and when I got home my Mum was crying and praying. "I told you, no swimming, no swimming!" There was a reason for her fear. Growing up in the city of Warri in Nigeria, Mum used to go swimming in the lakes and rivers near her house with her siblings.

One day, she and her brother were carried out by a strong current, and luckily she was saved by a man who grabbed her just in time. Her brother tragically drowned, leaving her terrified of history repeating itself. She was constantly worried every time any of her children went swimming, and it was a great relief to her when my childhood eczema meant that I had to avoid the majority of the mandatory swimming lessons at school. I only learned how to swim properly as an adult to take part in recovery sessions at the pool for my athletics career.

Sport is often the thread that binds children to their dads, and I was no different. Since arriving in the city, Dad had adopted Liverpool as his team and when I think of him, I see him happily cheering that brilliant side of Kenny Dalglish's on the telly.

Like every Liverpool family, the date of 15th April 1989 is seared on my brain, even though I was only a little girl of five. Dad was looking forward to a competitive FA Cup semi-final between Liverpool and Nottingham Forest at Sheffield Wednesday's home ground of Hillsborough and the whole day was dedicated at our home to watching the match. Mum, as ever, was busy in the kitchen, and I was her tiny sous chef.

Dad had been so excited about the game, but I remember seeing his mood change suddenly as he watched the screen. I was so young and couldn't fully understand what was happening and why the game was being delayed.

I eventually looked at the TV and just saw a sea of people swaying helplessly in the stands.

Thank God my young brain couldn't process that they were being crushed to death. Dad was speaking to Mum in Igbo quickly, explaining to her what was happening on the field, to shield the true horrors from me, my brother Chiz and my sisters Chika and Nkechi.

Mum started praying and then silently watched the

screen. I knew then that this was going to be a day like no other in Liverpool, or even after it.

The next day was completely quiet across Merseyside. You could hear the leaves rustling on the street where usually there would be crowds and cars on the road. It was a day of mourning that began a tireless fight for justice for the families who lost loved ones in Hillsborough.

Like every other family in Liverpool, we grieved for the dead, not only that day, but in the years that followed. At the most challenging times, you understood how close the people of Liverpool stood beside each other to provide support.

I loved to sit in the African hairdressers in Liverpool while my Mum was getting her hair done and listen to the chatter amongst the customers. There was tutting and nodding when concerned mothers and grandmothers worried about a potential match between families. Or worse, maybe a free-spirited son had decided to leave his accountancy course at university to chase his dream of acting.

A problem shared was a problem halved and the hairdresser would act as a confidante, dispensing wisdom between applying the hot comb that worked as a coarse straightener for black hair, listening to customers' voices that served as a Greek chorus.

The pavements in Liverpool are rarely dry and the cold wind can pierce your bones, but on those days, sitting in the hairdressers, I was carried back to the warmth of the Nigeria of my family and ancestors. I felt a strong connection to a land that I had never visited. I was able to begin the tentative first steps of discovering that I was British and loved my life in Liverpool but was of Nigerian blood and heritage that would ultimately define my life.

The majority of Nigerian immigrants had first arrived in Liverpool shortly after the country's civil war ended in 1970. Unlike Manchester, where young Nigerians often came to study at university, Liverpool's docks and factories attracted workers who had previously made their living on merchant ships.

Skilled Nigerian boxers such as Dick Tiger and Hogan Bassey also arrived in the city seeking stardom between the ropes and eventually brought world titles back to Merseyside.

Traditions from home were quickly brought to Liverpool by the first migrants. The community formed large families, not bound by traditional bloodlines, but by their rich connection to their homeland.

There was a family available from almost every part of Nigeria and if there wasn't one from your homeland, you would quickly be adopted.

The families were large and boisterous, filled with the familiar smells and sounds of a land far away. For special occasions, such as Christmas, the community would happily spend days moving from house to house and family to family, each place filled with food and laughter.

The Igbo Club and Community Centre is based in Toxteth, a racially diverse area of Liverpool. From the moment I walked into the Igbo Club as a young child, I felt happy and safe. I understood what my Dad meant by having an extended family in Liverpool. I was surrounded by aunties and uncles from every corner of Nigeria who I loved. From a young age, I operated in two different worlds, a Nigerian one and a British one. I was familiar with the sounds of the Igbo language that my parents communicated in frequently, and heard the words flow over intense debates in the centre in Toxteth.

The centre was the social heart for the Nigerian community in Liverpool and I loved to visit and take part in the dances held for children. Nigerian society is dictated by the community, and families look after one another. The Igbo Club ensured that no family went without during the tough times that came to the city under Margaret Thatcher's reign as Prime Minister.

Food was cooked for families going through hardship and support and friendship was extended to those who needed it. It was in this society that I was raised, which etched its values on my character forever.

At the Igbo Club, I was able to meet other kids with Nigerian parents and we were able to swap notes on our lives. The stories were rarely hugely different. In Nigerian expatriate communities throughout the world, studying hard isn't negotiable when living under Mum and Dad's roof. Education is prized because of the opportunities that it can offer, as well as the burning desire to prove that, as

Nigerians across the world, we are talented and hard-working. Homework was completed on time, exams were studied for with complete dedication, and watching *Sister/Sister* or the *Rugrats* on the telly was a rare and a prized treat.

Academic success at school for a second-generation Nigerian child was celebrated, not only by the family, but by the extended Nigerian community in Liverpool.

They were not just marks on a random school's report card; they were proof that the collective sacrifice of our parents in making their lives far from home had been worth it. We were able to prove that Nigerians could do things just as well, if not better, than their British counterparts.

I think back to those early days in Wavertree and smile, as it was so innocent and, to my young eyes, perfect even. I wanted those years to move slower so that I could savour every moment and enjoy it even more. The innocence of my early childhood was to change forever, with a simple move to a neighbouring suburb called Dingle, that was a short drive from the large family home that I loved and could have stayed in forever.

Things fall apart in life, the shattered pieces can be put back together, but the damaged fragments can ultimately still be seared in your mind.

2

Things Fall Apart

MY LIFE in Wavertree as a young child seemed to stretch out into a series of long sunny carefree days. I was young, innocent, and the fastest little girl in the street. Maybe I am guilty of applying my rose-tinted glasses, especially given the fact that sunny days in Liverpool are a rare thrill to be enjoyed amongst the wet and windy ones. I do know that I was truly happy and so was my family.

Dad continued to work hard at his financial career and found what he thought was a perfect house in Dingle. Mum had also become worried about our safety on the roads of Wavertree, where we were running wild and free. When my sister Chika was knocked over by a hit-and-run driver just after buying her Kylie Minogue and Jason Donovan *Neighbours* stickers from the local newsagents, the move was sealed.

Dingle offered a little bit more space, and on paper, it seemed like a smart move to an area that was potentially on the cusp of gentrification, offering good opportunities for buyers. At the age of 10, in the hot summer of 1995, I was sad to be leaving a house and neighbours I had grown to love but was also excited at the prospect of a new street to dribble my football down like my new Liverpool hero, Toxteth's superstar striker Robbie Fowler.

Our new address 73 Warwick Street in Dingle will always be imprinted on my mind, no matter where in the world I roam. I have accepted that I will never be able to outrun the haunting memories of Dingle. From our first day on the street, I could feel vicious hatred from a local gang of kids: the Onuora family were not welcome at all. We were used to being the only black faces in a world of white ones, dealing with microaggressions, such as being watched closely in the supermarket when buying bread and milk by the manager, but we had never experienced such naked hatred to our faces.

It started with long stares from these kids, not passing impolite looks of curiosity at the new black family in the street full of white people, but grimacing, hostile stares that dared you to say something in reply. The football games that I had loved as a child with neighbours in Wavertree were not going to be replicated in Dingle, and my ball was going to stay in the hallway unused. Chiz Junior and I had once cycled the length and breadth of Wavertree, mimicking Chris Boardman's gold medal winning ride for Britain in the 1992 Barcelona Olympics, but our bikes also began to gather dust in the house.

My Mum and Dad did their best to shelter us from the cold atmosphere outside the house, by creating a warm one within it, filled with as much love and security as they could muster. At 10 years old, I was on the verge of teenage insecurity and all the worries that go with it. My Dad always took me by the hand and simply told me, "Nika, you are absolutely beautiful, please never forget that." He was doing what any father would do for their anxious daughter, but he was also creating a security blanket for the world outside that was going to become increasingly hostile for me and my siblings.

Playing outside the house with the neighbours' kids being out of the question, we left the house for only two reasons; to go to school, or to go to church in the mostly white suburb of Mossley Hill with our family. Playtime would now have to take place within our back garden with my brother and two sisters. We would walk home from school with our heads down, aware that a gang of bullies could set on us at any moment, spitting savage racist taunts.

From our first weeks in Dingle, the bullying may have been racist and relentless, but it was rarely physical. Sometimes I wish that it had been a quick stinging punch from a bully with pain that would pass eventually. Instead, the racist insults of those years have never left me. The word "nigger" was spat at me countless times on the street, but it stung the most when a neighbouring gang who took particular pleasure in the torment cornered me. The boy who spat out racist bile at me with the most venom was of Chinese descent. I could see his bloodshot eyes and the spit on the side of his mouth as he shouted and swore at me almost in a manic trance. I remember looking at him with shock and fear in my eyes. Surely he knew how it felt to be different, so why was he the cruellest one in this group?

It doesn't take a child psychologist to work out that the psyche of a bully often works in a herd mentality, and it is far better to be at the centre of a vicious group than to be the one that suffers alone and helpless outside it, particularly if you could be next in the firing line for the bigotry.

My family were certainly alone in that street in Dingle and we were direct targets of a group of gangs with racism at their core. Their ruthless and relentless campaign of hatred was due to be ramped up a further notch.

Beyond the naked racist hatred that we experienced daily in Dingle, our street was also a hotbed of 'normal' crime. The local gangsters drove past with drug deals for neighbouring houses, or in high-speed chases with the police, or the 'bizzies', as they are commonly known in Liverpool.

One well-known gangster, Jimmy, lived across the road, and was constantly on the run from the local drug squad, creating some excellent viewing from the front window as he climbed over roofs like an acrobat to get into a safe house, performing his own hasty highwire act for the cheering locals.

The noise of police sirens and car tyres skidding became the soundtrack to our lives in Dingle, mirroring the constant tension that we felt. Although this gang of kids were ruthless in their pursuit of my family, the adult neighbours in Dingle never gave us any bother.

In fact, in between his circus skills dodging the bizzies, Jimmy took it upon himself to find the kids who were taunting us and sort them out for us. Jimmy's parents, Carol and Jimmy Senior always made sure to invite our family in for a few drinks every New Year's Eve. At the worst of times, the kindness of this family and other neighbours kept us going.

After the racial insults that my siblings and I regularly heard on the street from children, it was only a matter of time before the bullies got even more vicious. Our house provided easy target practice for the gangs' stones and bricks, with our windows regularly getting smashed to pieces. We were constantly worried that the bricks were going to be swapped for bullets.

In no time, not even Jimmy the gangster's daily dance with the bizzies on the rooftops was an excuse to go near any windows at the front of the house, it had become far too dangerous. The front of the house became an absolute no-go zone, due to the front window being shattered most nights by bricks and so we existed in the relatively protected back rooms. Mum and Dad were increasingly tense and worried, but still did their very best to protect us as best as they could by assuring us that everything was going to be ok.

Mum and Dad have a strong Christian faith that was passed down to me and all of my siblings, and perhaps they felt that, through grace, we could somehow weather this storm. We were taught that on the cross, Jesus said: 'Forgive them father for they do not know what they do'. The issue with these kids was that they knew exactly what they were doing to my family.

At that young age, I could tell that my parents were scared, not for themselves, but for their young family, unwittingly brought into this cesspool of hatred. I used to crook my ear to their door and hear them arguing in Igbo, their native language. I couldn't really speak it very well, but I could understand it all very clearly. My Mum was continually asking why my Dad had brought us to this area with so much fear and fury. Dad loved Liverpool dearly and simply couldn't understand how such evil existed on its streets.

At night, I developed terrors and became a confirmed insomniac. Today, I am sure I would have been diagnosed with severe anxiety. I didn't know what to call it then; I just knew I didn't want to go to sleep in case our house was attacked, or worse, firebombed. I used to listen to the soothing sounds of the British R&B group Eternal to calm myself.

While listening to Eternal's lead singer Easther Bennett's songs of redemption, I replayed the racist sneers from the local children that tormented my siblings and me every time we walked home from school. Mum and Dad could both snore for Nigeria and I actually used to find that sound reassuring and comforting in the middle of the night. I would lie just outside their room on the hallway carpet, knowing that they were near, and somehow, they would be able to keep our family safe. Eventually, I would fall into a restless sleep, broken throughout the night with visions of the gang attacking me with stones and words. I am not sure which hurt most.

Every Sunday, we would attend church; it was non-negotiable. We would all get in the car to travel to Mossley Hill to sit in a mostly middle-class white congregation. Dad didn't want to be segregated by colour and thought that in the house of God, of all places, we should mix with people of other backgrounds and be welcome.

At Sunday School we were taught the importance of forgiveness and love of our neighbours, while my family were surrounded by hate and venom in Dingle. 'Love thine enemy'? It was proving more difficult every day. I never minded church, which at least took us away from Dingle and provided some needed respite. I often wonder whether it provided me with an anchor during the long storm of racist abuse that my family suffered. However, the local gangs that took so much pleasure in harassing my family knew that we attended church every Sunday and that it would be the perfect time to strike with a memorable attack.

I was and still am extremely close to my Aunt Bisi. If you're ever in trouble, Bisi is the person that you call, and the issue will get sorted every single time. Whether I had messed up an exam as a kid, or later as an adult if there was a big problem in my athletics career, Bisi was the first number

I dialled. I was happy to spend Easter with my favourite Aunt and her daughter Sylvia to give me a break from life in Dingle. I am not sure why, but this particular weekend, I felt something was up at home and I rang Dad to say that I wanted to go home.

He said no, just enjoy your time at Bisi's and come back on Monday instead of Sunday, which I did, not questioning why he wanted me to stay an extra day.

On Monday I arrived home to see that there was no car and asked Dad where it was. He told me not to worry about it. Eventually, it came out that our one and only family car was completely burnt out in a racist arson attack by the local gang. Dad had kept me longer at Bisi's because he was scared for my safety. If they had blown up the car, what was to stop them going one better and burning our house down to the ground with us in it?

Contacting the police was pointless; we had learnt from bitter experience that they did nothing. It was just another group of delinquents or scallies as far as they were concerned, and the gang's determined and consistent racist behaviour didn't add any urgency to the case.

My parents tried their very best to shield me and my siblings from the worst of the panic and upset, but when your family's one means of transport has been firebombed, with no other motive beyond hatred at the colour of your skin, it is difficult to retain a balanced view of the world.

The innocent, rose-tinted view I had once had of life as a

young child happily playing in the streets of Wavertree was blackened forever in Dingle.

After the car was firebombed, the family home was not safe to be alone in at any time, especially on a Sunday. My parents constructed a detailed rota which meant that at least a few of us would be at home to try to protect the house when it was inevitably attacked again.

Every Sunday, just as the minister in leafy Mossley Hill was giving his sermon, our house would either be attacked or burgled by the gang. It became a horrifying routine. We knew that the front window was a no-go zone, as a brick could come through it at any time of the day or night.

The arguments between my parents escalated most evenings and I could hear my Mum and Dad shout at each other. It was always a loving and tender marriage where arguments were relatively rare, so I knew that they were under serious stress. Mum finally broke down to Dad after the car was firebombed and in her distinctive Igbo she cried, "Do you want your children to be killed, Chiz? Because I can tell you this is what will happen if we spend a single week longer in this house."

The big old house in Wavertree that had been filled with happy memories of neighbours and the extended Nigerian community, crowded in the kitchen over delicious smells and soothing music, seemed so much further than five minutes' drive from Dingle. I never walked in Dingle freely.

I was only too aware that I didn't deserve the racist insults

I was peppered with every time I walked home in my school uniform. I felt completely unwanted, and worse, unsafe, in my own home, due to the colour of my skin. I felt caged in a world that didn't want me.

In the summer of 1998, just before David Beckham got sent off in the World Cup and put on his snazzy sarong, we finally got the word from my Dad that we were going to leave Dingle. We had been there just a few short years, but the bullies had almost broken me psychologically and had left their legacy forever.

My family had received sticks and stones, and unfortunately, the words had hurt even worse, as my mind would retain their lingering sting for years to come. I crossed off the days until we left Dingle on a calendar, happily ticking off each day, like a prisoner awaiting parole from the Governor and willing their day of freedom to come sooner.

I am damaged by those years in Dingle.

I was brought up in a family with strict values that you should treat others, as you would want to be treated yourself. My siblings and I were raised with a strict belief in manners and respect towards everyone we met. When I grew up in Liverpool in the early years, I ran carefree in the streets of Wavertree, completely oblivious to the tense shackles that were going to be placed on me a few suburbs away.

I could sense the strain on the family, not only listening to my parents' late-night arguments in Igbo, but in the fear that I saw on my siblings' faces. We had all been happy children and this innocence had been robbed from us, through the hatred that had been inflicted on our family. However, the racism we experienced did succeed in bringing us closer as a family. We understood that when the world seemed against us, they could do anything, whether physical or mental, but we would stand closer than ever before. I believe the strong bonds that I have with my family to this day were truly forged in those desperate days of Dingle.

I returned to Dingle just once more. It was in my first week of school and we had moved to our new house in Wavertree not long before. I had bought eggs and stepped off the bus at the roundabout. I had studied the timetable all week and timed the bus to perfection, knowing exactly when it would come back to take me home.

I methodically egged every house where a bully lived. I threw each egg with all the power I could manage, happily watching the cracked eggshells and mess of yolks dripping down the bully's wall. Somehow, I wasn't caught by anyone, either by a gang member, or my God-fearing parents, who would have been horrified, regardless of the provocation.

After the last egg was thrown, making a sticky mess over the brickwork, the bus came perfectly on time and I sprinted for it.

"Jeez girl, you look like you're in a rush," the cheery bus driver said as I got on, completely oblivious to my handiwork minutes earlier. I cried tears of anger and sadness and left Dingle forever physically, but never quite mentally.

3

The Fastest Little Girl In Liverpool

THE SMART dark blue uniforms of my new secondary school, Archbishop Blanch, provided a comforting sense of order and structure to the chaos I frequently endured outside of the classroom.

Archbishop Blanch was a single-sex school and had a reputation for high academic results welcoming kids from all over the city, which pleased my parents greatly. Notably, the actress Kim Cattrall, who later found fame as Samantha in the TV series *Sex and the City*, had once briefly attended, before eventually swapping crisps in the canteen for cocktails in Manhattan.

Just like Dingle, I was often the only black face in a pile of white ones. The difference was that at school, I felt instantly accepted by a group of close friends, who continue to be by my side to this day. I had grown up in a home filled with Nigerian food, church on Sunday and the odd social occasion at the Igbo Club. For the first time, I was socialising extensively with a group of girls from across Liverpool, from a range of different backgrounds, and tasting the illicit, but delicious, Friday night 'chippy tea' at the local fish and chip shop when I could.

Mum and Dad understood that I would be exposed to western culture at school and encouraged me to make friends widely. However, once the door closed on the Onuora household, Nigerian values and food were what bonded us as a family and to move away from them would cause hassle. Like many children of migrant parents, I was a skilful social chameleon, able to switch personalities depending on the occasion.

Whether it was a big Nigerian wedding in the Igbo Club or a family dinner at one of the posher Liverpool suburbs with a school friend, I knew how to adapt seamlessly.

There was palpable tension in the streets of Liverpool after the brutal abduction of two-year-old James Bulger in 1993, and that lingered well into the late nineties. James was taken away from a shopping centre in Bootle by two 10-year-old boys when his mother had momentarily taken her eyes off her child. James was eventually murdered brutally by a railway line in Walton, with his tiny body mutilated.

Every parent's worst nightmare had come true, with no explanation available, beyond the demonic evil of the two child murderers, Robert Thompson and Jon Venables. Every parent in Liverpool felt extra pressure to keep their children safe after this horrific atrocity, given its utterly random and sickening sequence of events. My mother held my hand that bit tighter after the murder.

My friends and I would walk in close groups arm in arm after school, not merely as a sign of teenage affection or even loyalty to a clique of girls, but as an essential defensive mechanism against any attacks.

The school bordered Toxteth, and notably, its park, which was a favourite haunt for flashers, who would jump out of bushes sporadically and display their naked bodies to schoolgirls before sprinting off. There were also random abductions of young schoolgirls in the surrounding area. This was the world that we lived in. We were scared in private, but in the safety of the group, we laughed it off as just another day in Liverpool.

After the viciousness of my formative years in Dingle, when we moved back to the happier surrounds of Wavertree, finally, all seemed to be relatively well in the world. My focus was my friends and doing well in my school exams. My bedroom walls were plastered with posters from the pop music magazine, *Smash Hits*, which I faithfully queued for every week at the local newsagents. Posters of Mariah Carey and Eternal gazed down at me as I wrestled with that night's algebra equation.

There were some examples of sporting success in my family, notably from my older brother Iffy who played football for Gillingham and Huddersfield Town and eventually became the head coach of the Ethiopia national team. He is now the Premier League's first head of equality, diversity and inclusion.

Although I admired Iffy's ability as an athlete, I hardly saw him, as he was away at various clubs across the country throughout his career, and I had my own busy teenage life in Liverpool.

I still loved Liverpool FC, but from the comfort of watching them on the sofa and falling in love with the new generation of handsome footballers, nicknamed, 'the Spice Boys'. Jamie Redknapp, Steve McManaman and Phil Babb swaggered on the pitch, and off it, in their infamous and ill-advised white FA Cup final suits.

Unfortunately, these players never added any silverware to the very dusty Liverpool trophy cabinet of the 1990s. I was an armchair fan like most Liverpudlians, who wore either blue or red, but ultimately, I had little interest in playing serious competitive sport, beyond the odd game of netball or rounders at school.

However, I had started to gain a reputation for cleaning up the silverware at the annual school sports day. There was no clear reason behind my ability as a sprinter; it was just something I could do with ease, like maths at school.

At times, it seemed so natural, when I ran at top speed that I could barely feel my feet touch the ground and nothing else mattered. Things just flowed easily. At Archbishop Blanch school sports days, if there was a running event, I was almost always sure of winning it. I didn't train and I didn't have any special technique, but I knew that I was always coming home with gold medals.

I was a shy teenager, but for those few hours every year in the summer term, I was the centre of attention, and my Mum would proudly sit there draped in ribbons and rosettes from my latest hoard of trophies and medals. Every school sports day was held at the local athletics club track at Wavertree, adding a small sense of grandeur to the proceedings. We were finally able to compete on a real running track, with a small spectators stand on the side filled with cheering parents.

Neither my parents nor I thought that I could take my running further than my annual day in the sun at school sports day. The local coach from the Liverpool Harriers and Athletic club, Stan Roberts, attended most local school sports days across the city to work out whether there were any future stars he could add to his club's youth roster.

As a retired schoolmaster, he had an excellent network of teachers who would alert him to talented kids. Similarly to a football scout, Stan would spend lonely days and nights trying to unearth the next gem for his club. For the last three years, he had faithfully turned up at the track at Wavertree and unsuccessfully lobbied me to join the Harriers.

After another sports day where I had dominated all the track events, Stan found me while Mum was snapping a few commemorative photos of me posing with my medals and invited me to attend a club training session. He sidled over while I was mid pose for my Mum.

"Anyika, every year we go through this, girl," he said. "You were outstanding out there today and you'll probably be outstanding next year, but where is it taking you? You have a ridiculous talent, one that I haven't seen too often and I've been at enough of these bloody things to know it. It's time to get some proper training at the club, so you can really show us what you've got."

After listening to Stan, once again, I very politely said that I wasn't interested. I enjoyed my moment of glory once a year with Mum and the annual photo shoot with my bounty of medals, but that was it. It was one happy day a year, like a birthday or Christmas, but instead of wrapped presents I knew I was going to have shiny medals to hold. Sports day was a brief and happy distraction, but nothing more. I was more focused on my schoolwork and hanging out with my group of friends.

Incidentally, my school friend Michelle Molineux had started attending the Harriers' club sessions. From humble beginnings, this community club, driven by volunteers, has produced 53 Great Britain athletes and 16 of them have gone on to wear the national vest at an Olympics or a Paralympics.

When I was at school, the most notable Harrier was Diane Allahgreen, a powerful sprint hurdler, who competed at the Sydney Olympics in 2000. The club was set up thanks to the sacrifices of pillars of the Liverpool community, like Stan, who dedicated untold hours volunteering to allow locals to compete at the highest level possible.

When Michelle heard that Stan had asked me to come to a training session, knowing that I was shy, she promised that she would be there at the session and strongly encouraged me to come. I eventually agreed that I would go, but only if she would stay with me for the whole of the training session. I was entering a completely unfamiliar world, and I needed a friendly face beside me.

While I was the queen of the track at Archbishop Blanch school, across Liverpool, there was a sprinter who the other girls talked about with serious admiration. At the urging of my school, I had started to represent the school in the County Championships, where I was able to smoke most of my competitors with ease, but found a determined adversary in Vicky Griffiths, who would later compete as a senior athlete.

Vicky was everything that a teenage girl could want to be. Pretty, popular and effortlessly elegant as she won every track title in the Greater Liverpool area as a club athlete for the Harriers.

Unlike me, Vicky was a trained athlete who took her chosen sport seriously with gruelling sessions after school. She wore fancy spikes and sprinted against stopwatches; I just wanted to win medals for Mum at school sports day. I didn't know Vicky but wasn't sure I wanted to. I was quite happy to be unbeaten in school and wasn't looking to be up close and personal with a county rival from another world.

I have heard boxers talk about the smell of a gym the first time they walked in and how they were hooked on the sport for life, but that didn't happen for me in athletics.

I arrived at the club's track on a summer's night to find that Michelle had decided not to attend the training session at the last minute. There was drama to attend to on TV at Summer Bay in the Aussie soap *Home and Away*, and the windswept track at Wavertree could wait another day.

I had no mobile and no way to get home until the end of the session when my Dad would pick me up at an agreed time. I sat in the tiny spectator stand, completely decked out in the new training kit my parents had bought me especially for the training session. I was all dressed up with nowhere to go.

I looked down at the ordered group of athletes doing dynamic warm-up stretches to the barked and clipped orders of Stan who was evidently in his element. Stan reminded me of a kindly sergeant major in full control of his troops. Vicky was in the group, surrounded by a hovering group of adoring acolytes who hung on her every word and direction.

I decided then and there that this sport wasn't for me. I loved the proud look in my Mum's eyes every sports day, but winning those medals took little effort and I could run without a care in the world.

At the Harriers, it looked as if every footstep was choreographed and stiff. Surely the pleasure in running was to feel completely free? A strong wind sliced through the stand, cutting through my new tracksuit top like a knife made of ice. I tried not to be noticed and hoped that my Dad might be early to pick me up. I closed my eyes and thought about lying on the hot sand in Sydney with the cast of *Home and Away*, far from Wavertree, when I slowly gazed up and saw Stan standing over me. He wasn't angry, but he did have a puzzled look on his face.

"Anyika? We've been told that you were going to come down. Why haven't you started warming up?" Stan might have retired from the classroom, but the teacher's clipped tone remained. I told him that I wasn't sure if this was for me after all, and I was just waiting for my Dad to pick me up. "Well, you've come this far, and you've got your kit on," he began. "What have you got to lose by at least giving it a go? It seems pretty pointless to turn up and not even try something. It's your choice girl, either come out onto the track and warm up or go home. There's no point in wasting both of our time."

I finally made a last-minute decision to run onto the windy track and follow Stan.

That single moment as a teenager changed my life forever.

4

Ugly

WITHIN WEEKS of that first training session with Stan, I was part of the noisy and happy family at Liverpool Harriers.

There was an Olympian like Diane Allahgreen and weekend warriors who logged off their office computers at five and channeled their remaining energy into competing in club championships across the country. There was a new generation of talented young teenage athletes who were starting to make their mark, with myself and Vicky at the very front of the pack.

Across Britain, on cold Tuesday nights in the middle of November, there are countless unsung people like Stan Roberts, devoting themselves entirely to helping young people enjoy their sport.

I have a great deal of gratitude for the continued sacrifice that volunteers like Stan continue to make for little to no thanks; their only payment is seeing young people achieve their best, whether that is a faster time at a deserted club meet, or watching an athlete go all the way to the Olympics.

Stan was firm, but always fair and I responded immediately to the structure and discipline of his coaching. The design and dedication involved in the coaching sessions also appealed immediately to my parents, who knew that under Stan and the other coaches' care, we were completely safe at night training on the Harrier's track. After my troubled and tense years in Dingle, I finally felt free to run and do something I loved with new friends after school.

I realised quickly that while I was very fast, I was also completely wild in my running style. I was always an ordinary starter out of the blocks before using my strength to build up a steady train of acceleration.

Over 100 metres there was a game plan, where every movement was choreographed in an explosive dance that would strain every muscle to its base fibres and leave your chest heaving with exhaustion at the finish line.

I would sometimes hop the fence over the wall to training to avoid paying our club's subs to get into the centre. Any spare cash I had went on running kit that was treated with serious care. If I had the money, I was happy to pay my subs and the coaches would insist on taking me home at night if Dad was working late. The Harriers was my happy place, where for the first time I was able to completely shine outside the classroom.

I am not sure why, but the Harriers track almost always seemed to be freezing cold. I often wondered if Stan had persuaded the architect to make it just that little bit more open to the elements to toughen up his young charges.

I would try to make the best of it by telling the team that tonight we were to forget that we were in the middle of Liverpool, but to imagine that we were all sipping mojitos on the beach in the Bahamas. Anything to distract us from the biting cold.

While the wind sliced through us, I would be mockingly taking drinks orders from my bemused teammates. "Welcome to the Bahamas on another beautiful night in paradise. The stars are twinkling in the sky and all is well in the world. What are you having madam? Perhaps a Long Beach Ice Tea with an umbrella by the pool? Not a problem, I will get that sorted after our stretches."

Whether it was academic work, or sprinting, I worked best in a relatively regulated environment, where I knew that if I put in the hard work, I could see the results of my graft. Similarly to my dedication to my schoolwork, through hard work I transformed from a completely raw sprinter, to one that was beginning to be noticed in the north of England in the 100 and 200 metres events.

I was benefitting from training and learning from Vicky, who drove me to complete better training sessions every time we competed on the track. I didn't just want to emulate her, I wanted to beat her convincingly at every opportunity.

From a young age, I possessed a strong body that developed further as I entered my teenage years. Although my muscles would eventually help me develop into a world-class runner, as a teenager I hated my body. Within the walls of the Harriers, I was able to utilise my strength to explode out of the starting blocks and win countless titles as a sprinter, but outside the track, I felt ashamed of how I looked.

Every young girl and boy will have their own insecurities to deal with, especially under the microscope of cruel teenage schoolboy taunts in the playground.

I was lucky that I never dealt with any serious playground bullying, largely due to a close group of friends who provided a protective shield against any normal teenage nastiness that I could have encountered.

They reassured me that I was beautiful, and my Dad continued to tell me the same thing, but I didn't believe them. I looked in the mirror at my muscular, powerful thighs that were able to propel me to sprinting titles but couldn't make me love myself.

It was not only my body that made me feel different as a schoolgirl; it was my skin and hair. I knew my dark skin and hair stood out in the annual school photos. Every time I flicked on the telly, I would gaze at the pale skin of the 90's pinup Jet from the *Gladiators* TV show as she flicked her long silky hair forward, or the rich caramel skin of Destiny's Child in my *Smash Hits* magazine. I understood that no one the British public perceived as beautiful on TV, a billboard or in magazines, looked anything like me.

Despite my Dad's constant reassurances that I was

perfect just the way I was, I tried everything to change my natural appearance. First on the agenda was my hair which had a thick texture: I wanted it straight. My pocket money was drained by a product called 'Dark and Lovely', which used chemicals to 'relax' your hair to a straighter and silkier texture. I actually used to dream of looking like the girl on the 'Dark and Lovely' boxes. She looked perfect to me, with long flowing locks.

I wanted my hair bone straight and to fit in with the crowd. Kids used to regularly tease me in the playground because of my hair. Mum could never do braids properly, so sometimes it used to have a life of its own. Kids called me Whoopi Goldberg after the actress who had recently become famous for her big hair in the film *Sister Act*, or they'd call me Medusa, the Greek monster with snakes for hair, who we had just learnt about in class. I knew that my hair would mark me out as completely different, no matter how hard I tried.

Dad was caught between understanding the pressure I felt as a teenager to fit into British society however I could, while also maintaining his firm belief that I was uniquely beautiful and should be proud of my heritage. He told me I didn't need to ply my hair with layers of 'Dark and Lovely' to get it straight, but he also knew how hard it is to look African in an almost completely white society.

Without speaking a word, or giving a hint of our personality, our hair has marked us out as different.

My Hidden Race

Most teenagers rebel against the thought of conformity, but in reality, they just want to be part of a group. Some exceptional teenagers are brave enough to stand out from the crowd regardless of the consequences of their social standing, but I wasn't one of them. My friends did everything possible to make me feel that I could belong, but, despite their best efforts, I only had to look in the mirror to see my black skin and textured hair to know that I was different. I felt every inch the ugly duckling. Every time we would get ready for a night out, I wanted to share makeup, clothes and hair tips with my friends, but I couldn't. Instead, I would use the hot comb to make my natural hair painfully conform to what I believed was attractive in British society.

As a teenager, you need a strong anchor to weather the storm of insecurity and swirling hormones. I was lucky that I had three points of security – a loving family, close friends and an athletics club where I was free to express my talents. I should have been confident, as my junior athletics trophy cabinet started to grow, but I wasn't.

I didn't like the way my body looked and always wanted it covered. Before my sprint events for the Harriers and school, I refused to wear the short regulation gym knickers, I insisted on wearing a long and modest hockey skirt that I felt covered my legs and bum more effectively. I looked as if I was running to catch the Hogwarts Express with Hermione and Harry, not like a swaggering teenage sprint queen.

My days were always busy, filled with schoolwork and

the increasing demands of the track as my success grew. I was becoming a frequent visitor to my friends' homes whose families always welcomed me with open arms.

On Saturday outings into the city with my friends, I always secretly dreaded going to our regular hangout, the Tammy Girl clothes shop. I would try on dresses and while my friends would do their best to be supportive, none of them ever correctly fitted my body.

The dresses were all designed for a single shape, which was tiny and skinny. I was neither. I would look at my muscular legs straining through the seams of the dress and quickly retreat to the safety of the dressing room, often in tears.

One close friend had a Mum who could be relied on to hold the fort in case my parents anxiously called when we were on a night out. If my parents called asking where I was, she would tell them that we were busy doing our homework or watching a film and they would be satisfied. She also recognised my intense teenage dislike of my body and one day gave me a shopping bag and told me to open it.

I shyly thanked her and tentatively opened it to find a glamorous form-fitting red dress that wouldn't look out of place in any club in Liverpool.

After being urged to try it on, I looked at myself in the mirror, and for the first time, I actually liked what I saw. I slowly came out of the bathroom, to be met by mock wolf whistles from my friend's Mum. "Anyika girl, you look absolutely gorgeous," she said. "What did I tell you?

I have exceptional taste, and I can tell you one thing love, you're gonna be in serious demand for the school disco." I had purposely forgotten the annual school disco, a study in teenage anxiety if ever there was one. Girls spending all night getting ready, to stand awkwardly on the side of the school gym, while furtively watching the posturing boys that they fancied.

Boosted by a rare bout of confidence from my own personal shopper in the guise of my friend's Mum, I decided that me and my red dress would be going to the Archbishop Blanch disco which excitingly was being attended by the boys from St Margaret's school. My friends were all beautiful and had no shortage of suitors outside the school gates from the local lads, which did nothing for my confidence as I would always be left standing awkwardly at the side.

But, now, and for the first time, I noticed that I was getting more looks than normal from the boys. The hired DJ was making his way through a medley of early noughties hits, as the first brave boys started to do that awkward jog-cum-dance and initiate the first contact with the opposite sex.

Before long, a group of boys had approached our group. I braced myself to be left standing alone once more, when one of the boys suggested to his short, ginger and spotty friend that he should dance with me.

I had an inbuilt alarm system for mockery or sarcasm in any boy's voice and could detect none, he genuinely meant that it would be a nice idea for us to dance. There was a short moment of silence after he asked the question, before the boy said loudly, "Why the fuck would I want to dance with a black girl?"

The protective circle of my friends once again instantly enveloped me and the reluctant dance partner was left a crumbling mess by the insults that came thick and fast from the girls.

For my own dignity, I gave him a piece of my mind, telling him he was hideous looking and dancing with him was absolutely the last thing I wanted to do, but the damage was done. I had already become skilled at keeping up a strong appearance in the face of insults, but inside, I always knew that I was damaged badly.

The fragile faux confidence of the red dress had been brutally shattered. I went home that night, ripped off the dress and looked in the mirror, at my body, my skin and my hair and felt completely ugly.

I was different in every conceivable situation in my birth country and I was sick of it. I cried long into the night and wondered why I couldn't look just like my beautiful friends at school.

I was sick of being the black girl in a world of white people. I was sick of sticking a boiling hot comb through my hair and plastering my scalp with chemical relaxers to coax it straight. On the track, I was strong, free and, at times, unstoppable. Off it, I did not want to be out in front; I just wanted to be part of the crowd for once.

5

Mother Africa

WHEN I closed the door on the Onuora family home, I was in Liverpool physically, but never quite fully mentally.

In a cold corner of the United Kingdom, the customs and values that had been passed down from my family's ancestors over generations on the hot plains in Nri, Nigeria, continued to dictate how we lived our life in Merseyside. The food that we ate was exclusively Nigerian, which suited me as I adored it.

Every night we would feast on a range of delicacies like ground rice and egusi soup or my favourite boiled yam and stew. Mum was a skilful cook and warned me to never ever visit the local fish and chip shop as I would spoil my dinner.

Due to its strictly prohibited status in the Onuora family, the local chippy took on the mystical allure of a prohibition speakeasy for me. I didn't crave illicit booze, I simply wanted greasy takeaway food like any decent Scouser. The smell from the street used to torment me as I walked home. The owner had even been told by my Mum, in no uncertain terms, that me and my siblings were strictly banned from entering. Scared, he sensibly agreed.

The chippy tea is a prized tradition in Liverpool. Every Friday night, families will join a long queue outside the local fish and chip shop after a hard week grafting and then they'll feast on the wrapped treasure when they get home. Going home with my friends from school on a cold night, the intoxicating smell of fried food finally broke my resolve. I had finally had enough temptation and I wanted in.

I boldly went into the chippy, with the nerves of a teenager with a fake ID looking for cheap cider, and lying, told the owner that my Mum had changed her mind and was partial to a chippy butty after all.

I crammed hot greasy chips into my mouth before getting home, finishing them in a few minutes. I sprinted up the stairs to gargle half a bottle of mint mouthwash to cover the evidence from the crime. My mother was downstairs, but was blessed with the nose of a bloodhound and immediately sensed there was contraband grease in the house.

After some brief questioning from the prosecution, I folded, and Mum completely lost her temper. A rarity for her. You do not come between a Nigerian woman and her jollof rice.

Our social lives continued to be focused on church and the Igbo Club. We were taught the importance of manners, hard work and putting the community before yourself. Elders were respected and I found close allies in my aunties who would continue to support me throughout my career.

My ears were used to the sounds of Igbo that I would hear from family at functions as they discussed the latest activities at 'home' in the village. Still, standing on the damp streets of Liverpool, Nigeria remained a distant land to me.

Every summer, for as long as I could remember, Dad would return to his home village in Nigeria, where he would spend around three months with family. In Liverpool, he worked exceptionally hard to provide for his family. He often returned late at night on freezing evenings, after another hard day at the office. Dad believed that his responsibilities and obligations didn't stop with his family in the United Kingdom but also extended to his family in Nigeria.

There was a status bestowed upon Dad within the village as the successful migrant, who had achieved what some of his friends perceived to be the dream. He had a family, a good career and owned his own home in England. Reality and perception are of course completely different, and his family and friends from Nri didn't understand what it was like to be glared at and arouse suspicion in a shop simply because of your skin colour.

They didn't know what it was like to be randomly stopped by the police, as part of a 'random routine' and patted down by a needlessly aggressive officer, that somehow happened on a regular basis.

Dad would go home to where he was born and had spent

the precious formative years of his life to reconnect with his homeland, culture and family. He would bring countless suitcases stuffed with gifts, courtesy of Liverpool's varied auction houses.

Once he even packed a van with presents and shipped it to Nigeria. This was expected of him as the returning migrant, and requests would be fulfilled for items that could only seemingly be purchased in England. I never understood why a toaster bought from Liverpool was superior to one from Lagos, but I didn't write the rules.

Dad was building a large house in the village, and every year he would add another room. To be able to walk around the house, in his later years, on his plot of land in the village, surrounded by friends and family who had known him since boyhood, gave him the greatest happiness.

He had built a life and a family initially in Glasgow, before ultimately settling in Liverpool, but his childhood village of Nri would always be his forever home.

Mum and Dad wanted their children to experience what life was like in their home country and every summer one of my brothers or sisters would go and visit for six weeks during the school holidays.

At 15, with a busy life at school and on the track, I would listen to my friends' holiday plans with envy. There were holidays closer to home, maybe a caravan at Skegness, Centre Parcs for the more well-heeled, or even more exotically, Orlando, Florida.

After hearing about Disney World and the Epcot Centre from a lucky friend who had been there, after her Dad had blown the family savings on the trip of a lifetime, I got steadily obsessed with the idea of visiting Orlando.

I used to duck into local travel agents on the walk home from school to pick up a selection of the latest brochures for sunny Florida. With the rain lashing against my bedroom window, I would carefully circle the elegant hotels and pretend that I was planning to chase the sun this summer with a thick wad of green American dollars.

I was finally going to escape the cold at 15, but not to see Mickey and Minnie Mouse in Florida, instead, I was going to Nigeria for the first time.

I had spent my whole life in Liverpool, and apart from the odd trip to see relatives in London, I had barely been beyond Merseyside or even been on a plane. The world that I was used to was white, and within it, I was always the differentiating factor, whether that was at school or even on the athletics track.

When I boarded the British Airways plane at London Heathrow to fly to Lagos, Nigeria, I saw a plane filled with black Nigerian passengers and air stewardesses. I was alone and Dad was waiting to meet me in Lagos, as he was already with the family in Nigeria. Before the plane had taken off, I felt closer to a feeling of home than I had ever felt in Liverpool, where I had spent my whole life.

At the best of times, Murtala Muhammed International

Airport in Lagos is not for the faint of heart, but luckily, my Dad was used to its unique rhythm and pace. I clutched his hand tightly as we wove through the crowds and the noise to get my baggage. I waited by the carousel for our suitcases and looked up. The billboards selling Colgate toothpaste, Samsonite luggage, Guinness and Coca-Cola all had beautiful models with gleaming white teeth.

For the first time in my life, I saw that every model staring back at me from the huge glossy posters was black. For once, I didn't feel isolated. I was in a country where to be black was beautiful and celebrated, not hidden away for fear that you could be singled out. I stepped into the warm sun of Lagos and readied myself for the long journey to Dad's village.

The journey to Nri in the Anambra region of Nigeria takes nearly ten hours through winding roads and it gave me enough time to get acquainted with the country through the car window. When I had told a girl in school that I was going to visit Nigeria, my excitement was tempered by her reaction. "Why the hell would you want to go there Anyika?" she had asked. "I've seen it on TV and I'm telling you it looked horrible. It's seriously poor and they said you can't even drink the water. Can you not tell your Dad that you want to go to Centre Parcs instead?"

For the majority of British people in the 1990s, and perhaps even now, Africa meant intense poverty. Forget Africa being a cradle of ancient culture and civilisation; no, Britain had been fed on a diet of malnourished African babies on the 9pm news, coupled with Bob Geldof yelling at them to donate.

I do not pretend that poverty doesn't exist in Nigeria, but it is a small part of one of the most fascinating countries in the world. Naija is a land of steep contrasts, from city to country.

There is the heaving metropolis of Lagos, filled with hustle and excitement, and the calm and lush countryside, where cocoa farmers and their families toil all day in the unforgiving sun. It is a country rich with natural resources, with some of the most industrious and intelligent people you will ever meet. With each bump and turn in the road, my eyes were wide open, and my mind was absorbing every detail of the land of my ancestors. Dad was smiling in the front seat of the car throughout the whole journey, happy to be home at last.

We arrived in Nri late at night in inky darkness to be met by a procession of relatives. We were ushered into my Grandmother's house to escape the crowds, while relatives welcomed me to the village. Before leaving for Nigeria, my Mum had bought me a really nice camera to capture all of the trip, but she had given me strict orders not to give it to anyone, family or not.

I didn't understand what she meant, but after the long ceremony of greetings, Dad started emptying several suitcases filled with goods bought in England. Toasters, weighing scales, kettles and radios were taken out and distributed amongst smiling relatives. Dad reminded me of Bruce Forsyth on the old TV quiz show *The Generation Game*, with a conveyor belt of assorted goods for the lucky prize winners.

I had my camera out for a second to capture this scene when a cousin asked me if she could have it. She didn't want to borrow it, she wanted to keep it. Her tone was matter-of-fact, without any sense of embarrassment. We were visitors to the village from abroad and it was expected that we would bring gifts. Remembering my Mum's words about the camera, I told her no, I was sorry, but I couldn't give it to her as it was a present. She looked confused, and Dad – wary of keeping the peace with the extended family – immediately told my cousin that it was fine and gave her my camera.

Only days later, after a tirade down a crackly telephone line from my Mum in the Igbo Club to my Dad, was my camera returned.

Dad was home in his village, but ultimately, he was always going to be the favourite prodigal son. Never quite settled in Liverpool, yet never fully embedded back in Nri either.

On the first morning, I was woken by my Granny before the village cockerels had sounded their cawing chorus. There was work to do, not only in the house, but in the village, and honoured guest or not, I was expected to help out.

I had grown up steeped in hard work, whether it was at my academic work or on the track and began to understand where my parent's mindset was forged. In Nigeria, if you do not work, you might not eat that day. From 4am, everyone in the village started work, with clearly delineated roles between men and women.

The men went out to work in the fields, or in whatever industry they were involved in, while the women were expected to look after the children and ensure that every matter in the household was taken care of, from cooking to cleaning.

Granny tried her best to teach me the perfect way to prepare her favourite recipes, but somehow, I could never fully master them to her exacting standards. There was a rigid code of family values that you did not dare move from, you respected your elders and did what you were told.

The British world champion heavyweight boxer Anthony Joshua spent a period of time as a pupil at a Nigerian boarding school and understands, as I did, how strict family values come first and foremost in the country. "It was a change," he remembered. "5.30 in the morning, up fetch your water, put like an iron in your water to warm it up. Your clothes had to be washed and ironed. In the [Nigerian] culture it's family, outside support; everyone has a role in raising the kids."

Alongside the strict hierarchy of the family, there was intense joy at meeting a huge part of my family that I had never met in person before. Far from home, long before Wi-Fi, I was fully immersed in village life, listening to my family's stories of my parents when they were younger.

There was a warmth and generosity that meant if you were family, nothing was too much trouble for my relatives.

They would do anything to ensure that you felt happy and welcomed. Stan Robert's strict training regime in Liverpool seemed far away as I feasted on mounds of starchy Nigerian stews every night under the stars.

I was always extremely close to my father, and really, a Daddy's girl. I believe on that trip that our bond grew even closer as he was able to show me the land and family that he loved so dearly.

He was able to show me how far he had come in his life, in terms of what he had reluctantly given up in family support and love, to gain the educational and professional opportunities for his family in the United Kingdom. Dad was always happy in Nri, surrounded by those who had known him since he was a boy. He invested countless amounts of time and money in the house that he was building, not only for himself, but for the extended family to use. In Nri, the long hard days of work are for a single purpose, to provide for your family. Everything in your life is dedicated to the betterment of your family.

My grandmothers thought nothing of the sacrifices that they had made to ensure that their son and daughters could thrive in a far-off cold island. Standing barefoot on the warm earth of Nri, I understood that, as happy as I was with my family, I also had a life that I loved in Liverpool. I was caught in a quandary that would never get solved. I was too westernised to be considered fully Nigerian, but in Britain, too black to ever be completely accepted.

6

Lighting The Flame

IN SEPTEMBER 2000, the leaves were falling on wet Liverpool pavements and the evenings were getting shorter as I returned for another year at school.

My unhappiness at leaving those rare balmy summer evenings of training at the track was softened slightly by seeing the sun shining at the Sydney Olympics on the television. I had watched the previous Olympics, but none hooked me quite like the Games in Australia's beautiful Harbour City.

My training at the Harriers had gotten a lot more serious, and at 16, I was recognised as one of the best sprinters, not just in the north of England, but in the whole country.

I was a regular winner at the junior club athletics leagues, ironically sponsored by McDonald's. I never considered that athletics could be a sustainable future career, but I did understand that I now had the potential to take this sport to an extremely high level. Quite what that level would be, I didn't know. I was just driven by a relentless passion to run.

My clubmate, Diane Allahgreen, had been selected to compete in the Sydney Olympics for Great Britain in the 100 metres hurdles, and suddenly, it made the impossible feel within reach. It was a long way from a humble club track in Wavertree to a packed Stadium Australia but Diane had done it.

At the Harriers, Diane would stretch with us and pass on words of advice, or simple encouragement that would make your week. Athletics is unique in that it is a common sight to see elite Olympians limbering up in training with juniors and weekend warriors in clubs across the country, inspiring everyone differently.

At night, I established a ritual with my Dad where we would stay up late into the night and watch all of the events where Great Britain had a chance of winning a medal. We would sit up with blankets over our knees as the BBC began their coverage, sweeping over the sparkling blue water of Sydney Harbour, to showcase our medal hopes that night.

Sitting at home in the sitting room in Liverpool with a cold wind blowing outside, springtime in Sydney felt far away, but mentally, being able to watch Diane competing, I wondered exactly what was possible and where in the world my talent on the track could take me.

The Sydney Olympics is remembered fondly as the most successful British Olympics for medals won since the 1920 Games. After the relative failure of Atlanta four years before, Britain won a total of 28 medals in Australia, 11 of which were gold. I was hooked on every athletics event possible, but also found myself screaming for Britain in rowing, boxing and cycling when gold medals were won.

Dad would doze off between events, but then suddenly wake with spectacular timing, just as Steve Redgrave and Matthew Pinsent won an incredible gold in the coxless four rowing. Audley Harrison's gold in boxing and Jonathan Edwards triple jumping to the top of the world, after silver in Atlanta four years before, also kept us wide awake and cheering into the wee small hours.

I remained unashamedly a Daddy's girl, and these late-night Olympic marathons were precious time between us. A shared love of sport can often draw children to their fathers that bit tighter, and we were no different.

At home with his daughter in Liverpool, far from Nigeria, Dad was passionately cheering for his adopted nation and maybe secretly wondering if his daughter could one day grow up to join this select gathering of the world's greatest athletes representing Great Britain.

In an iconic Olympics filled with British medal winners, one athlete stood out more than any other for me, the heptathlete Denise Lewis. Few events demand more of an athlete mentally or physically than the heptathlon and Denise's gold lit a flame in me that has never been extinguished. We competed in completely different events, but it didn't matter. I had never seen a black female athlete look so powerful and strong, yet also effortlessly beautiful and graceful.

After the Olympics, Denise did an iconic photoshoot for *Total Sport* magazine where she was photographed with blue body paint, mimicking her Olympic outfit. Denise was proud of her strong body and when I saw her take on the world and win in Sydney, I wondered why I couldn't follow her example.

I remained uncomfortable about the way my body looked, particularly on the track, and in Denise, I saw a powerful and muscular black woman who radiated beauty inside and out. Beyond her incredible performances in Sydney, Denise was also admired for her intelligence and analysis off the track, which brought her event to life.

Fans hung on her words as she eloquently described the pain of competing with injuries on the way to her heroic gold in Australia. In the same way that young boys in the playground would pretend to be Michael Owen scoring goals for Liverpool, at the track, the young girls, black and white, suddenly wanted to be like Denise.

After the Olympic flame had been extinguished in Sydney and inspired by Denise, I worked even harder on the track and the following year won the English schools' intermediate 100 metres title in Exeter in front of my Dad and my brother Chiz Junior, who had driven five hours south to see me.

I managed to win the title without using starting blocks. I won from a standing start and my competitors who all used blocks thought I was engaging in Muhammad Ali levels of sporting psychological warfare to show my dominance.

Little did they know that I simply didn't know how to use starting blocks properly. That race also provided me with my first prize money, with the Royal Air Force generously donating £300 in Selfridges vouchers.

The largesse of the Air Force allowed my cousin Jacqueline and I to briefly live the high life with a personal shopper in London, sipping tall champagne flutes of orange juice as we tried on the latest Calvin Klein jeans.

The school's title also allowed me to wear my first Great Britain vest in an Under 19 international against France in Dole, a small pretty town not far from the Swiss border. I almost wasn't picked.

My cousin Amala was also a sprinter and I had gone against her in the English schools, beating her. When she was picked ahead of me, I was surprised, but congratulated her anyway and focused on my training. A few days after selection, I received a call from a very apologetic UK Athletics official, telling me they'd put down A Onuora, thinking that it was me.

After a short call, I was told they'd like me to come and compete and were still going to keep Amala in the team. Dad was hovering at the side of the phone and was ecstatic when I told him I'd been selected. He spent the evening ringing every Onuora family member from London to Lagos at great expense to tell them that I was going to be representing Great Britain in France. In many ways, life had come full circle. The sacrifices that Mum and Dad had made as migrants had allowed their daughter to represent the land they now called home.

Despite their great pride, Mum and Dad were nervous about me leaving for France. I finally had a mobile, and Mum gave me strict instructions to drop call her so they'd know it was me.

Eager to impress at my first international event, I proudly turned up at Birmingham Airport decked out in my full international tracksuit and noticed that everyone else was casually dressed in jeans. I ducked into the bathroom to change quickly, feeling like the kid at school who had forgotten it was non-uniform day.

Like most teenagers, I was confident and comfortable around those who knew me, but the thought of travelling to a tiny town in France with a bunch of strangers from all over the UK made me nervous. Would I be able to understand the Belfast and Birmingham accents? More worryingly, would they be able to understand my Scouse accent?

After arriving at the Dole Athlétique Club, with its pristine track and small whitewashed grandstand, I quickly clicked with my new teammates, who were actually fairly seasoned international junior athletes and used to these international events.

It felt a bit like a fun school summer camp, staying in a dormitory in the middle of nowhere, chatting late into the night, but with a high-octane international athletics meeting as our chosen activity instead of horse riding and crafts. I felt

I was in a safe space, amongst young black British girls like me, who had experienced the same prejudice, dealt with the same pressures on appearance, and lived to push themselves to their limits in their chosen sport.

I got close with one girl from east London immediately, who like me had Nigerian parents and understood the pressures off the track to succeed. Her name was Christine Ohuruogu, and even as a teenager with big dreams, it was easy to see that she was destined for success at the highest level of the 400 metres. Christine was easy company, and we laughed at shared experiences of growing up in a Nigerian household or when a new teacher in school butchered our surnames reading out the roll call.

All most people see when they see my name is a string of vowels, and their brain starts spinning into a panic, and Christine had the same issue. I had too many As and she had too many Os for most tongues to pronounce correctly.

Yet, once she got on the track, Christine had an ability to switch into an almost Zen-like focus and became an unstoppable competitor who had also competed regularly as an England international in netball.

Christine and I were inseparable on that trip, and it was the start of one of the most important friendships in my athletics career. Competing in Dole, I came second, with a time of 11.86 in the 100 metres, which promised that I would have more opportunities to wear the coveted international vest in the future.

It was my first time touring with an international team and I didn't want the experience to end. Although I was blessed with a strong group of friends at school, through competing in Dole, I found teenagers my age who completely understood the life that I was living, with all its challenges. I had a brief taste of competing for my country and I wanted more.

In life, we look endlessly for close friendships, and I was lucky in Dole that I met people who continue to enrich my life. I was part of a group of young female athletes, united by their fearless desire to be the best that they could possibly be, and willing to smash any obstacles that came their way.

Whether it was racism, or sexism, which would rear its head against us in years to come, we were far stronger as a unit. In the most individual and, at times, selfish of sports, I had found a sisterhood and a best friend in Christine.

7

Growing Pains

AFTER SCHOOL, I did what any teenager with Nigerian parents would do. With my Dad's encouragement, I signed up for a sensible degree in economics at Liverpool's John Moores University.

My interest in economics was at best negligible, but there was no way that my parents were going to give me their blessing to devote my life to the track without further qualifications and I didn't want to give them an unnecessary early heart attack. I was selected for the European Junior Championships at 18 and knew that to get further in athletics, I would have to live like a nun clad in lycra.

There are few better places to be a student than in Liverpool, it's just a shame I didn't experience any of it. The city is friendly, fun and incredibly affordable, even on a measly student budget. Students arriving in Liverpool can have the night of their lives on just over a tenner, and still have change for a kebab and a taxi home. Student bars outdo themselves with themed nights and cheap drinks offers, gaining loyal customers every September at the start of term. I saw all of this, but from the vantage point of the university library. I didn't even allow myself to enjoy a single wild night out in Freshers' Week. I was utterly committed to being the best athlete I could be.

I had a wide circle of friends, both in athletics and outside the university, but I made a conscious decision as a student that I was going to let nothing derail my progress in athletics. I look back at my student days and I sometimes wonder if I couldn't have let my hair down a bit more, but I was setting the standard for the success that would come later in my career, just when temptation was at its peak.

I knew that I would make little or no money out of athletics, but it didn't matter. I was driven to compete for my country in the Olympics and, whatever it took, I would get there. I had changed coaches at the Harriers, from Stan Roberts to Morris Condon, father of Sydney Olympian Allyn, who later switched from sprinting to the bobsleigh, appearing in the 2010 Winter Olympics in Vancouver. Allyn had been part of the British 4x100 metres relay team in Sydney, and I wanted to be coached by a man who knew how to get me to the Olympics. To do that, I knew that I had to live a life less ordinary.

My days and early evenings were filled with training in Liverpool or physical therapy in Manchester. During the day,

I was engaged in a practical study of physics, as I tried to work out how to use enough force to propel my legs over 100 or 200 metres in the shortest amount of time. By evening, my spikes were swapped for heavy textbooks, with thrilling titles like *Financial Theory and Corporate Policy* or worse, *Post-Keynesian Economics* and I would work late into the night doing my essays and revision for impending exams.

I got to know the library security guards well, as they saw me sprinting to get in just before they closed the door every evening. I can't say that studying economics was a labour of love, but when I have decided to do something, I must do it to the best of my ability.

It is the work ethic that has been instilled in me by my parents and my family in Nigeria. I would sit in the library with only a few sleeping students for company and see my friends returning home from a crazy night out at 2am.

They'd bang on the library window, press their faces against the glass and beg me to come out for a nightcap at a house party nearby in the city centre. I would smile, stick on my headphones and return to my books. I wasn't a normal athlete, and I wasn't going to be a normal student either, I had to be the best.

I was also juggling my academic and track work with demanding daily shifts in the Moat House Hotel to pay for all my physio, international trips and equipment. I had three separate plates spinning quickly; university, my job and athletics. Any one of them could crash down at any moment.

Sadly, the Moat House was demolished years ago, but in its day, it was where the great and the good would come when they visited Liverpool. John Travolta, Dame Judi Dench and any number of Premier League footballers were known to stay there. Famously, the huge 250kg professional wrestling star Yokozuna died in the hotel of a lung blockage during my normal room service rounds.

I had worked in bars throughout my teenage years and had refined my banter with customers to an art form, all designed to get the maximum return in tips.

If it was the office Christmas party circuit at the hotel, I was the first to sign up for extra shifts, knowing that the leery and lairy accountants who had indulged in too much house white vino would be more than happy to throw me a few extra Christmas coins with their latest large drinks order.

One customer I had who was staying in the hotel ordered a vast amount of food to his room and always insisted on settling the bill with thick wads of cash, insisting that I keep the massive tips. This customer was unusual in that he was local but was staying in his room for over two weeks and not leaving it.

Although I was happy with the extra cash that could go straight towards my training expenses, I was immediately suspicious. The man's room was a mess, with piles of cash stacked everywhere. Don't forget, I had grown up with a ringside seat watching Jimmy's run-ins with the bizzies due to dodgy drug deals and now I wondered if I was dealing with a Scouse Pablo Escobar, with a unique fondness for bacon butties at all hours of the night.

My suspicions were ultimately proven right when I came up to deliver his food. He invited me into the room and asked me inside to put the tray on the table. I ended up putting the tray on a huge mound of cocaine by mistake, which set him flying off in a rage. However, I stood my ground. "What the hell are you doing having a massive pile of coke in here when you're asking for room service?" I demanded.

I wondered if I was going to get murdered for being a witness to vast proceeds of crime. I didn't stay for the response. When I went back to tell my manager, it turned out that the piles of cash that he was paying the hotel with were fake and not long after I delivered the room service, he fled the hotel in fear of getting caught by the police or a rival drug gang. It was just another mad day in the Moat House.

Dad would often insist on picking me up after a long evening shift to make sure that I got home safe. He was always a careful driver, so one night after he picked me up, I was surprised to see blue lights flashing and signalling for us to pull over.

Dad stopped the car and through the mirror I saw a male and female police officer come to the side of the vehicle. The male officer was immediately aggressive, rapping on the window strongly with his knuckles and loudly demanding that Dad get out of the car. "Sir, I have reason to believe that you have been drinking and would like to question you further," he barked through the window. My Dad rarely drank alcohol, he would sometimes have a small glass of Guinness at Christmas, but that was about the height of it. He was more or less a teetotaller. Dad didn't say a word, he simply nodded calmly and did what he was told. Just before he got out of the car, he turned to me and looked into my eyes. "Nika, listen to me; no matter what happens out there, please just stay in the car and stay calm," he said. "Leave it to me. Ok?" His words and behaviour told me that he had been in this situation many times before.

I did what I was told, watching my Dad while this male police officer jabbed his finger in his face and yelled at him. I knew there was no crime to investigate, it was just an opportunity to exercise a bit of power against an innocent black man who had the audacity to drive his daughter home from work.

Eventually, I couldn't stand it any longer. I was sick of watching my kind and dignified Dad being treated like a piece of dirt on the officer's shoe, just because of the colour of his skin. I got out of the car and I immediately heard my Dad telling me to go back. For once I ignored him. I was charged with a rare anger that comes from watching injustice happen before your eyes that is accentuated when it involves those you love dearly.

I walked straight up to the police officer and asked what the hell did he think he was doing. "You've just dragged my Dad out of the car for no reason, and now you're trying to tell me he's drinking? He doesn't even drink. He was picking me up from work, so unless you're damn sure that you haven't pulled him over for no reason, I suggest you let him go right now." There was a moment of silence. Dad looked at me stunned and the male police officer visibly shrank.

Finally, the female officer stepped forward, quietly apologised and said it was fine to go. We got into the car and drove home. Dad said that he was proud of me, but also upset at what I had witnessed. I had seen racial profiling from people who were meant to protect us. My Dad had done nothing wrong but somehow, had found himself as a black man in the wrong place, at the wrong time and needlessly harassed by the police. What about the other times this had happened when I hadn't been there? Was this harassment from authority the expected tax that he had to pay for living in this country as a black man?

Back on the track, I was the only female member in Morris' coaching group at the Harriers and I was now training with seasoned athletes. Morris was a lovely man who dedicated his life to coaching voluntarily, outside his normal demanding job as a social worker. He had taken his son Allyn to the Olympics and the World Championships and I thought that, with this coaching, there was no reason why I couldn't do the same.

The sessions were tougher and made harder by Allyn's constant sniping in my ear when I found myself crouched down in agony after another gruelling session. "You're soft girl," he would say. "You're going to have to harden up, I'm telling you Dad, you're going too easy on her, talent only takes you so far in this game."

I admired what Allyn had achieved as an athlete on the world stage, which had come through sheer determination and grit. Like Diane, he had shown all of us at the Harriers where hard work and talent could take you if you wanted something bad enough.

You could move from a suburban track in Liverpool to the Olympics. But, unlike Diane, I didn't warm to Allyn on a personal level. Maybe he was trying too hard to be the bad cop to his Dad's good cop to motivate me. Or maybe he was just a bit of a prick.

Regardless of his son's unwanted tough love, Morris was the perfect coach for me as an ambitious junior athlete. Nothing was ever too much trouble for him, frequently paying out of his own pocket to look after his athletes, including once paying for me to get on a flight home after I missed one back to Liverpool from an event abroad. He refused to take the money I owed him, just telling me to put it towards my training expenses. That was Morris, who, like Stan, devoted hours of his time and energy for precious little thanks.

His reward was seeing his training group compete to the best of their ability and that was all he ever wanted.

Morris loved athletics, but hated the politics that surrounded the sport, particularly from its governing bodies filled with starchy and stubborn old men. He frequently warned me, "Anyika, UK Athletics will stab you in the back if you let them. Always stay on guard." Morris had an ability to take an aspiring athlete to the Olympics, but he wanted no part of its bullshit boardroom dramas. I didn't understand his words then as a bright-eyed junior, but in years to come, they would make perfect sense.

Other things, however, did not.

To cope with the increased demands that the higher intensity training was putting on my body, I would visit a host of different physios in order to try and stay as healthy and as injury-free as possible. At night I was a student of economics in the library but on the various different treatment tables I would lie on, I really became fascinated when they talked about biomechanics. My body was a strong and powerful one, but like a finely tuned engine, it could be seriously temperamental when pushed slightly the wrong way.

At one point, I was suffering from a lower back and hamstring injury when I was told that one of my regular physios wasn't available for the next number of treatments due to a hectic work calendar. I was not too concerned by that, I was happy to see any physio and explained to the replacement exactly what was wrong with the tense muscles in my back and my tight hamstring.

I was dressed in my normal treatment kit of running hot pants and a crop top as I lay down on the treatment table.

The new physio started to feel my lower back muscles and explained that this was a common issue for sprinters, due to the amount of force that I was putting through my legs when I exploded out of the blocks. It was a consultation between an experienced medical practitioner and his patient, and I almost allowed myself to lull into a daydream, as I enjoyed a precious period of rest before a mountain of training and studying that loomed later that day.

Just as I was fully relaxed and he moved to my hip, explaining the frequency of tense hip flexor muscles in high-level sprinters, he placed his hand directly on my vagina. He did it calmly, while talking in a knowledgeable medical drone about my injuries, giving no indication that this behaviour was anything out of the ordinary.

My previously prone body was jolted into an involuntary shudder of panic, like a shock of electricity. My mind unravelled. 'What is he doing? Is this what I think it is? It can't be. Could it? He is an experienced physio. Calm down. They don't just hire people like that, you're overreacting.'

I lay there and after my body had flinched, he removed his hand from my vagina, before continuing the treatment and again, slowly pushing the boundaries whenever he could. For my lower back, he climbed onto the treatment table, and mounted me, saying that he needed to get more leverage to release tight muscles with his hands.

I could feel his erect penis through his trousers on my body, and immediately felt completely violated, but helpless. He knew that I would not or could not complain, so I lay still, in shock.

Unfortunately, I ended up getting physio from this therapist on several other occasions when nobody else was available. I would plead with the receptionist as to whether there was an alternative physio and was told there weren't any others available. When he pushed boundaries, I played a monologue in my mind that maybe it was standard medical procedure. It was only when I spoke to a friend who worked as a physio much later and explained the treatments that I was told, in no uncertain terms, that I had been sexually assaulted several times. I was in tears that day and for many after it.

I have never told a single person about this episode.

How many young female athletes at every level of sport have been sexually assaulted by a medical practitioner they trusted? When you are young and filled with dreams as an athlete, you are at your most vulnerable. Your job is to perform and conform. I was young and just making my way as an athlete with dreams of making the Olympics, I didn't want to rock the boat, even slightly. Who were they going to believe, an athlete with no name or a respected physical therapist? Did I want to go through reams of protocol and paperwork to protest that I had been sexually violated? Did I want to potentially put myself through a lengthy court case? Did I want to be splashed all over the newspapers? Did I want everything I had worked for in athletics destroyed?

The answer was always no. Like so many young women before and after me, I chose silence and self-preservation over the truth.

Larry Nassar, the disgraced former USA and Michigan State College Gymnastics team doctor, thrived on trust, building a rapport with the young gymnasts that he treated, who were competing in a brutal and unforgiving world of pain and diets. The gymnasts would go to Larry for treatment on their battered bodies and he would give them soothing words of kindness. He would even sneak chocolate and sweets to their rooms. All of these actions carefully built unbridled trust between Nassar and the gymnasts. Nassar acted as the friend they needed in a cruel world where only a gold medal mattered. He used this trust and viciously abused it, sexually assaulting hundreds of young women. Like me, so many of them never told a soul. Who would believe them? The medical professional had numerous years of experience and letters after his name. Nassar could easily explain any sexual assault as a routine medical procedure just as my physio in Manchester had done.

I was a young woman and dreaming of making the Olympics when I was first sexually abused. I tell this story now, for the first time, in the hope that it gives other female athletes who have been degraded and damaged in this way the courage to reach out and speak up. There can never be any excuse for this depraved and abusive behaviour, it shouldn't have happened to me and it shouldn't have happened to so many sportswomen who were abused when they were at their most vulnerable.

It sickens me now and it sickened me then.

8

An Apprenticeship
In Spikes

IN 2006, at the age of 22, I had my breakout year as a
senior athlete. I was selected in the 100 metres for the
Commonwealth Games in Melbourne and also for the
European Championships in Gothenburg. I won silver in
both events as part of the 4x100 relay teams. My parent's
mantelpiece in Liverpool now had some serious bits of senior
silverware to join my school's titles. My passport began to
drip with the ink from stamps across the world. I was starting
my apprenticeship and began to become familiar with the
rhythm of life as an international athlete.

Athletics generates hundreds of millions of pounds
in lucrative sponsorship deals, appearance fees and prize
money, but like most things in life, this bounty only comes to
a lucky few. I was at the bottom of the totem pole, and to be
honest, was simply happy to be competing at a senior level.

On the track I was guided by Morris but off it I was largely alone, plotting my own travel and accommodation through a complex sea of logistics and global races.

I did manage to get my first agent after the Commonwealth Games. If you have any interest in British athletics in the 1980s and 1990s, you might have heard of the late Andy Norman. Andy was the man behind some of our greatest athletes. Linford Christie, Jonathan Edwards, Steve Ovett and Fatima Whitbread, his wife, were all under his wing at some point. Andy was a former policeman and helped to steer athletics into the slick, professional operation it is today.

Andy had his enemies in the sport, but he was always brilliant with me. In a stiff world full of bigwigs and bureaucrats, I enjoyed his complete lack of ceremony and Del Boy wit. He would insist on paying me with wads of cash after events. He was like the *Deal or No Deal* ladies, with a briefcase full of banknotes. I remember once competing in Norway and forgetting to bring my kit. Andy told me not to worry, took me to an expensive sports store and told me to fill my trolley with whatever I wanted. The bill came to 350 euros, I asked him how I was going to pay him. He told me that as long as he had a receipt, someone would deal with it.

For the majority of athletes, our chosen gig is a seriously precarious financial existence. You travel to events in the hope of getting on the podium to generate enough prize money to take you to more events. Like a prize fighter hoping for that one big payday eventually, you compete at small-town shows to build your name and bank account slowly. The obscure Belgian town in Oordegem became a favourite haunt because I knew I would always run a fast time at its event. There are numerous obscure events like it dotted all over Europe, which you try to discover before your competitors start clocking fast times too, like an intrepid explorer armed with running spikes.

I arrived at the dead of night in out-of-town airports and travelled to the event's basic hotel to find out which athlete I was sharing a room with. It was always a moment of bated breath. When you start your career, you are completely at the mercy of the event organisers and their Russian roulette approach to room sharing. There is no straightforward logic behind the room selection, although I often got a difficult deal, sharing with someone with limited English.

Both my roommate and I would regularly be tied in linguistic knots as we tried to communicate who wants to shower first and if it's ok for me to watch *Desperate Housewives* on my laptop without headphones. I have shared rooms with slovenly sprinters, quiet distance runners and a particularly burly German shot putter, who always insisted on puffing on cigarettes in the bedroom while standing completely butt naked.

I make few demands of my new roommates, but when I arrive into the bedroom, I always go for the bed closest to the door. I am not sure why I do this, but ever since I've been a professional athlete I do it. It's part superstition, part habit and partly because I need to have easy access to the toilet in the middle of the night. I also insist on moving the beds as far apart from each other as possible. I have woken up in the middle of the night and gazed involuntarily into far too many shot putters' eyes before.

This is part of the deal of being an international athlete, we bed hop around the world, just with none of the fun that you might expect. You know that you are so lucky to visit places that you dreamt about as a little girl, like Florida, or South Africa, but once you get into the hotel, you are there strictly for business. The scenery might be nice, but it's utterly irrelevant to what you are there to do, which is to get on the podium and win some prize money that will keep your career going for a little while longer.

I am making very little money, but at this stage in my career, I honestly don't care. I love the sport and can't believe that I get to travel the world doing it. I never went into athletics to be rich; I am simply driven to perform at my best. I am told that travel broadens your horizons and largely it does, even if I see very little beyond the hotel and the athletics track. I travel almost always alone, which can be exciting, but can also leave me completely vulnerable when I least suspect it.

Since childhood, my life has been dedicated to being the best athlete possible. I never miss a training session, I diligently watch my diet and arrive at the track completely focused on the job at hand. My discipline wavers only once thanks to my passion for acid jazz, and one of its foremost pioneers, the British band Jamiroquai. I have become hooked on their music, and the lilting voice of their lead vocalist Jay Kay. I get an opportunity to see them live in London in a small intimate gig at the launch of their new album *High Times*.

The problem is, as normal, I have training scheduled in the evening with Morris. I pride myself on my commitment, and nobody respects Morris more than me, but nothing is going to come between me and seeing Jay Kay bouncing around the stage in his crazy collection of hats.

I tell Morris that I am not feeling well, and sneak down to London, arriving outside KOKO in Camden in the nick of time. I end up partying backstage with Jay, having the time of my life. I get a rare glimpse of life outside the strictures of my sport, and I love every minute of it.

In early 2007, I travel to the beautiful city of Bergen, Norway, for an indoor event in the 60 metres. I am looking forward to visiting this beautiful city, surrounded by fjords and mountains, but am focused on building some strong early form ahead of a gruelling season. I tend to keep myself to myself on flights, happy to grab some precious sleep ahead of the controlled chaos of international athletics.

I am dozing on the window seat when I feel something strange on my arm. In that half-dazed feeling between sleep and consciousness, I wonder if it is a burst of air from the vent above me. I slowly open my eyes and see that the man beside me is licking my arm.

I instantly recoil in disgust and anger. I ask him what the

hell does he think he's doing and he calmly looks at and says, "I want to know what a black girl tastes like."

I don't have the words to reply. I am young and scared, I don't know what to do, so I stand by the loos for the duration of the flight until it's time to land and I am forced to sit there frozen beside him. When I look at him, I see complete nonchalance, which tells me that he has almost certainly done this to black women before me and will do it to many after me with absolutely no fear of repercussions.

A year later, I am competing in Cagliari in Sardinia, doing some warmups before the Terra Sarda event, just outside the hotel on the grass. I am doing my warmup strides in my tracksuit when I see an elderly Italian woman watching me closely from her balcony. I briefly flatter myself that she might be an athletics fan, like the German and Dutch devotees who now come up to me and other athletes at events around Europe, with their scrapbooks packed with photos of every conceivable competitor, hoping for autographs.

Maybe this Italian Nonna is interested in the science of sprinting and is about to impart some wisdom on my striding before my race. The flashing blue lights of the local Carabinieri soon dissuade me of this notion.

Two police officers get out of the car, and in broken English, tell me that a neighbour had called them to say that there was a black girl trespassing on their property. In full athletics kit doing strides, I explain that I am competing in the stadium around the corner and show them my accreditation.

The officers apologised, but I knew that I had to stay calm. If I show even the slightest bit of anger, I risk getting thrown in the back of a police car in a foreign country. I am scared, humiliated and confused. I go out onto the track and perform terribly. The coaches will never know what happened before I put on my running spikes.

I get used to being followed in supermarkets across the world by staff, immediately judged as a potential shoplifter due to my skin colour. I ask white teammates to accompany me as often as possible, not mentioning that I am afraid of getting humiliated in the shop, but simply passing it off that it will be good to have company on the walk over. This is the world that I live in as an athlete, carrying a burden that isn't of my making and with nowhere to turn for help.

When something like this happens to you as a young black athlete, what do you do? I had nobody to talk to at a leadership level in UK Athletics, no one who understood what I had experienced or indeed the countless other black athletes who had worn their vest over decades.

There was no black representative at the executive level who we could talk to about racism. The track was dominated by black British athletes, but the boardroom was filled with white men in well-tailored suits. We couldn't see it, so we couldn't be it.

I knew that I wasn't alone in experiencing this racism as a British athlete, yet it was never spoken about seriously at leadership level. See no evil, hear no evil. Harden up and

Left: Mum and Dad's wedding day in August 1980

Top: One of my favourite pictures of me and Dad taken on Christmas Day, 1984

Above: Me and Dad with my siblings Chika and Chiz on Christmas Day, 1984

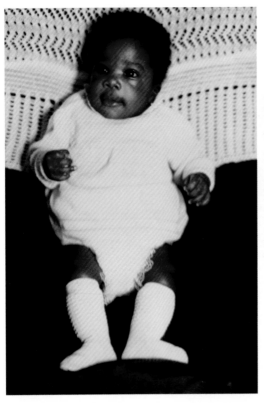

Above: My mum holding me on our way inside the Anglican Cathedral for my christening in April 1985

Above: Baby Anyika at three months old in December 1984

Left: Mum and Dad before a night out at the Igbo Club, Liverpool 1987

Right: Pictured with my big brother, Chiz, aged three in 1988. I was always attached to him when we were kids. I followed him everywhere. He was smart from a young age (as well as sometimes troublesome) and taught me everything from a young age including learning how to drive as a teenager

Above: Me and my younger sister, Nkechi, taken at Morrison Primary School, aged nine

Above: A family photo celebrating my mum's graduation and, frankly, my dad would find any excuse to have a picture of us all together. He was obsessed with photos and creating memories with me and my siblings. Left to right; my young sister Nkechi, brother Chiz, Mum, Dad, sister Chika and myself

Right: School photo aged 13, taken in 1997. At this point, my focus was purely on school. My unearthed sporting talent followed not long after....

Right: Competing at the annual school sports day in either 1999 or 2000, at Wavertree Athletics Centre. That was the day Stan Roberts scouted me (again) after winning countless medals. I decided to join Liverpool Harriers the next day and never looked back

Below: Archbishop Blanch School class photo, taken in March 1999

Right and below: Competing for GB at a U20 GB vs USA meet at Northwood Stadium in August 2001. Another great stepping stone at the start of my career. USA were always the athletes to beat as they were one of the best teams in the world and I relished the opportunity to compete against them

Below: A Team England International Schools Competition in Tullamore, Ireland, in July 2001. After I became English Schools Intermediate 100m Girls champion, I was selected to represent England at the annual Home Nations competition. I won my 100m race – despite food poisoning – and we won the relay event too

Above and right: My first GB call-up aged 16 at the U18 GB vs France athletics event, July 2001 in Dole, France. I was so excited to run well in the 100m. It was the first of many and such a huge honour to compete for my country at a young age

Left: A rare night off from studying and running round in circles. Me and my school friends went to see Craig David in concert at the Royal Court Theatre, October 2001. It was his first UK tour and I was obsessed with his first album, *Born To Do It*

Above: Myself, Joice Maduaka, Emily Freeman and Emma Ania celebrate silver in the 4x100m relay at the 2006 European Athletics Championships in Gothenburg, Sweden. Winning two global medals that season was a great start to my senior career

Above: Dad, me and Mum at an awards evening at the Anglican Cathedral celebrating my silver medal from the Commonwealth Games in Melbourne, Australia, 2006. I almost forgot about the event as I was in university all day and didn't have time to get changed, hence the jeans and hoodie!

lace up your spikes, it's time to compete and get the gold. There were coaches and competitors who were focused on the track and results, not on supporting black athletes when their spikes were off. You're a young athlete who is proud to represent your country, the last thing you want to do is rock the boat, so you say nothing.

I would sometimes talk about the lack of representation of black executives and support with my fellow athletes, but not often. We were walking on a tightrope made out of dental floss. If you spoke out too often and too loudly, you were scared that when it came to difficult decisions on funding or selection panels you'd dug the first few inches of your own grave as an athlete. You had fought hard enough to make it to this level and you weren't going to jeopardise it easily.

When I did speak with fellow black athletes about representation, we learned to speak quietly. We talked a lot about the need for perfection. We knew as black women competing for British Athletics you could never have a bad day, a bad session and certainly not a bad season. You arrived at the track every single day ready to fight for your future.

Many of us strongly felt that the system was never there to support you as a black woman.

Throughout my time representing my country, there wasn't a single mental health support worker within the system from a diverse background. There was always a desperate need for someone who not only provided clinical excellence, but also could truly understand the prejudices that we had encountered long before we arrived at the track.

After years of waiting and lobbying, the 4x100 women's relay team finally secured a sports psychologist in 2010. She wasn't from a diverse background and was quick to tell us that she had lots of black friends, but in the main, we really valued her support and advice.

If anyone wanted to grab time with her, the office door was always open. Generally, through her sessions she kept us calm and composed, allowing us to compete at the highest level.

In a standard relay catchup, the atmosphere changed forever. We had to complete a number of personality questionnaires, to work out what motivated us in this team. There were standard questions, the kind most of us have probably come across on a corporate team building day. Then, out of nowhere, the sports psychologist asked the two white members of our team a question.

"How does it feel to be white in a team surrounded by black girls?"

The question hung in the air like a bad smell. There was complete silence from everyone and eventually the whole team left the room, leaving the psychologist sitting alone.

My head spun first with shock, then with rage. I couldn't understand why someone so experienced and qualified would ask something like this. She had basically made it clear that she was uncomfortable with black women and saw colour before talent. She had needlessly isolated one group of women from another based on her own unconscious bias.

As a black woman you live in perpetual fear of being labelled loud, aggressive or cocky. We have heard it since we were at school, so many of us choose to keep our heads down, for fear of offending others. So often a black woman with an opinion is considered a threat.

The sports psychologist in question went from having a bulging roster of clients down to a trickle. Teammates white and black felt uncomfortable with her after the incident and our team never worked with her again.

Off the track, I am beginning to understand the complex business of sports marketing, which is some reward from all those late nights in the uni library studying economics. You are not only running quickly to win medals and bank prize money, but you are also competing hard to get valuable shoe contracts. I am delighted as a young athlete to be sponsored initially by a company that is a pioneer in advanced running technology.

I am conscious about my body shape and I almost always choose to wear black or dark colours. I wear these colours because I believe that they will stop me standing out. They send me outfits in vibrant colours that I love in peach and pink, but when I try them on and look in the mirror, I start to cry. I do not want the harsh lights of stadiums to accentuate my curves and muscles. I always put in an extra order for more dark grey, brown and black clothes as a result of how uncomfortable I feel.

Right before the British Championships in 2007, I am asked to do a shoot for a catalogue with another athlete, the 800 metres runner Sam Ellis. I am worried about doing the shoot, feeling bloated from my period and unhappy with my body, but Sam is easy company and helps me feel at ease.

After thousands of shots of Sam and I in various bits of gear, we say goodbye, glad that our short-lived careers as models are over and we can return to the track. Months later, during a quiet moment at home, I pick up a catalogue to see if there's any gear that I might like for the upcoming season.

I spot Sam in familiar poses across the pages and search for myself, finding that the gear I was wearing has been reshot with a white female model. Sam, I should also add, is white.

This is the world that I have grown up in, since I was reading my *Smash Hits* pop music magazines as a little girl and seeing the adverts in it as a teenager. As a society, we have been conditioned, through our media, into thinking that being black and African is not attractive, so why should a sports company be any different?

Sports brands will stress that they do use black athletes in their marketing, but inevitably, it will be a mixed race or racially ambiguous sportswoman, who they believe is more palatable to their audience than a black athlete with classically African features.

This is not to detract from the racism and discrimination that mixed-race athletes experience as a result of the colour of their skin on and off the track. They experience the same hurt from racism that I have done. Yet, when we talk about diversity in sports marketing, are we truly reflecting the full scope of the Britain that we live in today in terms of representation?

It's not just an issue of race in the sports companies that surround athletics, it is also about how women are treated off the track through their contracts. How many times have I seen a talented athlete left with a basic shoe contract, while a perceived more physically attractive runner, with less talent, is emblazoned across catalogues and posters.

You realise that, to succeed, you are meant to not just run fast, you are expected to look good doing it. I know women who have been told to wear shorter and tighter clothing at events by race directors. I even know women that have been asked to sleep with the men that control the big races across the world, knowing that it might get them a favourable lane if they endure the sordid casting couch.

Athletics is a man's world and the rules are dictated by them in polished boardrooms far from the tracks we toil on. The incredibly talented USA athlete, Allyson Felix, who I had competed against in the 100, 200 and 400 metres, wrote a damning opinion piece in *The New York Times* about her sponsor Nike, regarding their poor treatment of her while pregnant. While pregnant, Nike offered her a 70% pay cut, when she asked them to contractually guarantee that she wouldn't be punished in the months surrounding childbirth if her performances dipped, Nike declined.

I have known athletes who have had voluntary abortions to compete at championships, because they fear that having a child will lose them the opportunity of a lifetime. Is this a logical world to live in? Female athletes who are pregnant have had to tread carefully, fearing that the career they have worked so hard to build could be destroyed forever.

After Allyson's article, Nike announced a new maternity policy for all sponsored athletes, with new contracts which guarantee an athlete's pay and bonuses for 18 months around pregnancy. This is great, but why did Allyson have to write her story in *The New York Times* to get reasonable protections?

We consume inspirational adverts from sports brands that tell women to chase our dreams and be the best that we can be to a pumping soundtrack, yet it's a thin smokescreen that fails to obscure the reality of the boys' boardroom.

Actions speak far louder than words and while it's always good to see change from sportswear brands, I question whether there are tangible actions beyond the creative facade of rousing ads?

I get selected for the World Championships in Osaka, as a late call up for the 4x100 relay team. Unfortunately, I am not picked for the team that will arguably never have a better chance to medal at a World Championships, being beaten to third by the Belgian team.

At 22, I know I have time on my side and I am happy to soak in the atmosphere in Japan, a country I love at first sight.

Apart from the Commonwealth Games, this is my first major championships, where I am seeing athletes from Nigeria and Ghana regularly, on and off the track. I find comfort in their poise and beauty. West African names like Kemasuode, Ojokolo, Osayomi and Amolofo roll off my tongue easily. I find comfort surrounded by athletes that look like me, rather than always feeling out of place and isolated. These women are my competitors, but also my compass in terms of confidence.

I am sick of walking carefully for fear of stumbling into another act of racism against me, but I am left with no choice. I have done nothing to deserve it, but regardless, I am a frequent victim of distrust and even hatred because of my skin colour.

Actions do not always need to be openly bigoted to cause maximum hurt, I have been left in the pouring rain by enough taxis while they swerve to pick up white passengers to know that.

The racism that I experience as an athlete across the world isn't my fault, but it does become my problem to deal with, and mine alone.

We suffer in silence and must deliver on the track regardless.

9

The Tests

MY FRIENDSHIP with Christine Ohuruogu remained as close as ever. We had been joined at the hip as bright-eyed juniors in France and continued in the same vein as we began our senior careers.

Although I was doing well, wearing the England and GB vest at the Commonwealth Games and European Championships, Christine was a rare prodigy in the 400 metres from the starting gun of her senior debut.

In spite of the success that came to her quickly, Christine remained the same grounded girl that I had known as a teenager in France. No matter what was going on in her life, with gold medals coming thick and fast at the highest level of our sport, she would always make sure to check in for a chat to see if there was anything she could do for you as a friend.

Christine had an amazing gift as an athlete. She had a switch that would send her into a deep focus on the track and in training, but away from athletes she was completely unaffected by the pressures of the sport. She was relaxed and carefree, with a pile of interests away from athletics, a complete contradiction of the single-minded athlete often mythologised in the back pages of the newspaper.

In the ruthless world of athletics, I was glad of her friendship, which helped me to navigate the difficult early years as a senior athlete. While Christine was getting used to gold hanging around her neck, I was just getting used to competing at an elite level. After gold in March of 2006, at the Commonwealth Games in the 400 metres, Christine had arrived on the global stage in Melbourne, only to be suddenly pulled off it.

Christine was banned from athletics for a year after missing three random drug tests, starting in July, not long after her 2006 triumph in Australia. As athletes, we must tell authorities where we will be for one-hour slots each day. If you miss three tests without a valid reason, you could be banned for at least a year.

After missing two tests, Christine made sure to text her whereabouts, every day, apart from one day when she forgot, then the testers duly came to visit her, and she wasn't at home.

Throughout the year of Christine's ban, I did everything I could to support her. I wasn't afraid of getting into arguments with fellow athletes or even friends and did so regularly. I believe her reasons for missing the test were nothing more than forgetfulness, and I stand by that. The Court of Arbitration backed it up in their ruling stating:

"There is no suggestion that she is guilty of taking drugs in order to enhance her performance or otherwise and, indeed, this case can be viewed in all the circumstances as a busy young athlete being forgetful."

Christine served her ban and went on to win gold in the 2007 World Championships in Osaka in the 400 metres, to be greeted by a front-page from *The Sun* trumpeting the headline: "Don't make this the face of 2012" across her smiling image.

Even after Christine's stunning gold medal run in Beijing, it never seemed enough to eliminate the doubt in some people's minds that she was a cheat and fraud.

Christine's year-long ban was difficult to witness as a friend, especially as she was in severe physical pain from a nasty achilles tendon injury.

You want to reach out and provide comfort, but you know that your words are largely meaningless. You see a friend getting broken by a rabid press pack that loves nothing more than tearing down a talented black athlete at the first opportunity. I stood up for her then and I will continue to stand up for her now.

When you are at home skimming the news and you read about an athlete missing more than one test, your suspicion of wrongdoing immediately jumps up a few notches. Bang the judge's hammer and pronounce them guilty. I don't blame you, if I hadn't been in the sport, I would be of the same opinion. I despise people who take performance enhancing drugs and have been cheated out of enough precious prize money and podiums by dopers. Some have been caught and served their bans, others got away with cheating throughout their careers and retired covered in garlands.

It doesn't take Scotland Yard to work out that an athlete who has been consistently sprinting the 100 metres over 11 seconds throughout their career, who then joins a coach who has been previously embroiled in controversy and is now comfortably running 10.8, may have some serious questions to answer.

However, proving that an athlete is a drug cheat is a difficult exercise, fraught with legal risk – just look at the case of Lance Armstrong – and in athletics, there have been famous cases where drug cheats have been caught and it is the clean athletes who are left embroiled in the legacy of their actions.

Unfortunately, it is almost never quite as simple as an athlete missing a random drug test meaning that they are deliberately taking performance drugs. I am not saying that it has never happened, but it is not as clear cut as the media would portray it. I should know, in 2017, I managed to miss four random tests within a chaotic month. I have never spoken about it and the missed tests thankfully escaped the clutches of the media.

Random drug testing becomes part of your life as an athlete, no matter where you are in the world. We update our details about the smallest change in our movements, they are then registered to a system called 'whereabouts'. Every week, you also must update a daily hourly time slot where you must be available for testers to come.

The testers that come and visit you become as routine and banal as the milkman or the postman, you even get to know some of them. There was a lovely Scottish couple who lived in France that did a lot of the European events. I got to know them so well, I'd even time their tests for fun to see if they could beat their 20-minute record. They come in, take your blood and urine and then you forget about them for a while.

My coach Rana Reider was based at that time in the Dutch National Sports Centre in the town of Papendal. Towards the end of my career, I was doing workouts sent by him in Loughborough, but would often find myself needing to do stints in Holland for intensive training camps. I had decided to travel to Holland and stayed at the track's on-site hotel for two days.

Then, trying to make things as cheap as possible, I was staying in an Airbnb, before having to move out into another apartment near the track. All of this was normal life for me, and I was extremely careful to update my whereabouts in the computer program so testers could locate me.

Once you've done the hundreds of tests that I have done over my career, it becomes just another part of your life. It is only when you miss that random visit for completely innocuous reasons that your life and career can be turned upside down. I missed my first test on 6th June 2017. I remember it vividly, as I had done my due diligence, and put my address where I was staying in Holland, including the apartment number in the additional information section of the location tracker. The tester turned up between the hours of 0703 and 0807 and was unable to locate my address.

I was at home and had done all the right things. I later found out that my address on the tester's database didn't have my correct apartment number due to a system glitch. There was a tester knocking on a random door, while I was sitting on my sofa oblivious that I had missed a test.

When you have missed a test, within seven days you will receive a letter and an email.

There is no immediate phone call or email to warn you and if you've missed it through a human or clerical error, it's just tough luck. The testers will almost certainly return quickly and they did. Except, completely oblivious to the first missed test, I had forgotten to update my address past 6th June in Holland, and the testers turned up my normal home address in Loughborough on the 8th and 9th June.

After the flurry of three missed tests, I received an email from UK Anti-Doping (UKAD) on 12th June, which had gone straight into my junk mail.

Skimming through my email one day idly I found it and my heart nearly broke through my ribcage, it was beating that fast through my chest. My first reaction was panic that my career could be over, or at the very least my reputation would be destroyed through the media. I had made a genuine error and a stupid one, failing to update my location when travelling to Holland for training, but also the system hadn't updated my address details accurately.

When I finally updated my location details for Holland on the 14th, completely oblivious to the testers circling, I was in Holland in the apartment at the agreed slot on the 16th, but there was no ringing of the door which apparently started at 6am.

It turns out the tester had turned up at the front door outside the apartment complex and was ringing the doorbell with no joy. In a subsequent report from the tester, they admitted they found difficulty finding the right apartment, but were assured that the one they arrived at was mine as a neighbour had pointed directly to my door, saying that there was a girl there with, I quote directly from their report: "Dark skin colour, who can run fast," living in it.

The testers could have walked past the front door now my neighbour had opened it, and knocked directly on my door on the ground floor, but they didn't. I sat there watching reruns of *Frasier*, completely oblivious that I was heading for my fourth missed test.

Thereafter, UKAD were really trying their best to locate me for testing; arriving at my home on Sunday 18th June at 8pm unannounced, which wasn't in my agreed time slot, which was 8am-9am. I wasn't at home, I was out for dinner with a friend in Holland, but, thank God, I got a phone call from the couple I was staying with, telling me someone was at the door asking about drug testing.

I could have argued that they were in the wrong testing spot, and I was being nailed to the wall, but I couldn't argue, I put down my cutlery and sprinted home to take the test.

If you have three strikes, and UKAD don't find your reasons compelling, you are facing at least a one-year ban with your reputation completely destroyed. As athletes, you are contending with your form, that will make or break your season and your livelihood. On top of that, you are on planes, trains and automobiles travelling to events across the world. It sounds glamorous and the wailings of the first world, but the EasyJet and Ibis Budget Hotel merry-go-round can lose its glamour fairly quickly.

It is absolutely possible to not be tested for months and get lulled into getting sloppy with updating your exact whereabouts, especially when 99 times out of 100, the testers will not be there for a random test during that week.

Should I have forgotten to update my location for two dates on the 8th and 9th June? Of course not. I was annoyed at myself for not updating my whereabouts in Holland, given that organisation is normally something I pride myself on. But we are talking about a simple human error that can absolutely destroy a career and reputation.

While the case was going on, I didn't sleep. I feared shutting my eyes and falling asleep in case the testers came and I missed them. My anxiety wasn't just centred on the case, where I was confident that I had made an honest mistake. I was also concerned that word would get out that I had missed a series of tests, because once that happens as a black athlete, you are guilty before the grand jury of the British tabloids. I had seen it all with Christine who was mercilessly torn apart by reporters.

Conversely, when countless white athletes have doped in a myriad of sports, we are often fed a story of redemption after a simple, yet fateful mistake. I have competed against enough convicted cheats who have walked back seamlessly into the starting blocks without a single outcry from the press. They have served their time, others don't get that luxury.

During the case, I was still competing and trying to get back to full fitness and form after tearing my hamstring at the Shanghai Diamond League. You might have seen me announced and I'd smile into the camera as it panned across the athletes. My smile was a thin veneer, given my stomach was constantly in knots, as I worried that my career and reputation would be shattered with no way back. I could write the tabloid headline myself, "Scouse Athlete Misses Drug Four Tests on Final Straight of Her Career."

I was in Paris for the holding camp for the 2017 World Championships in London when I saw an email that told me my case was being brought before a panel. Just before my last major championships, when I should have been focused on relay tactics, I was thinking about my defence.

I was getting ready for one of my last days of training,

with the music blaring, when I just about heard Neil Black, the UK Athletics Performance Director, yelling that there were testers outside waiting for me.

They had arrived at 7.30am, not my agreed slot of 9am, but it didn't matter. I was on high alert and couldn't afford to miss any tests whether it was my fault or not. I quickly finished my test with the Scottish couple who were once again in and out in record time. Throughout this whole ordeal, I never told my coach Rana about any of it. Just before I walked out to compete in London, I was fiddling with my app to ensure that my location details were absolutely accurate.

I was lucky, after a fairly rigorous and detailed defence, my case was considered and UKAD only considered the two missed tests that were genuinely my own error, when I had forgotten to update my address while in Holland. Another missed test and my career would have been ruined and my legacy tarnished, all because of forgetting to type two lines on my smartphone.

Cheating in sport through doping appalls me, it has damaged the sport I love irrevocably in some cases, particularly through the state sanctioned doping of Russia in athletics. However, while we need to take every case of potential doping seriously, there can be a simple human explanation for missed tests that we refuse to consider, instead of basking in the venom that hits the athlete in the media.

Christine dealt with unnecessary vitriol throughout 2006, and even beyond, in spite of her achievements as one of

Britain's greatest ever athletes. She had shoulders strong enough to take the unfair abuse and keep moving on to bigger and better things. It so easily could have been me, with the added bile of more social media tools for the trolls to call me a cheat and a fraud. I was just lucky enough to be able to prove my innocence behind closed doors in front of UKAD, far away from the poison pen of the papers.

10

The Majors

MY FIRST Olympics was the Beijing Games in 2008. After watching the chaos and brilliance of the Athens Games in 2004 on television with my family, I was determined to be picked to travel to China. After a blistering year in 2006, by the next year, I had almost become complacent without realising it and my competitors had caught up with me. I did just enough to get onto the Olympic 4x100 metre relay team squad and made my way to Macau for the Team GB holding camp.

Macau is known principally as the gambling hub of China and I felt that my cards were finally coming up as I entered the plush hotel where we were staying. After my early years filled with cheap hotels and red-eye flights, I finally felt that I had arrived as an Olympic athlete. Princess Anne visited the team and I bumped into her on my way to breakfast, completely unprepared for this Royal visitor. Forget courtesies, rigid protocol or tiaras, I met Princess

Anne half awake, giving her a friendly Scouse greeting of, "Hi, ya alright?"

Once I had composed myself into some form of royal decorum and Princess Anne had adjusted to my Scouse accent, we got on famously, chatting happily for ages before I politely excused myself to beat the breakfast rush. The Olympics is a wonderful, but completely bizarre experience from start to finish. After being kitted out with a stockroom's worth of branded Team GB kit, you are also given the team sponsors' bounty, which can be anything from a huge flatscreen TV to a basket of fruit.

When you arrive in the Olympic village, imagine Times Square and Piccadilly on acid, packed with thousands of the world's most talented athletes from every corner of the world and you will get a fairly accurate picture of what awaits you. The food hall becomes the social hub of the village and I'd find myself happily sitting there people-watching, never knowing who was going to pop in.

I meet people from all walks of life today and when they ask me about my career, the first question I always get is: 'what is it really like in the Olympic village'? I could tell them about the unlimited McDonalds you can gorge on, the bounty of free sponsored goodies or the opportunity to meet athletes from all over the world, but they're generally only interested in the sex. They've feasted on tabloid stories and they want to know if the athletes get it on with one another most nights and the answer is, yes, of course they do.

I always had a boyfriend, but I saw plenty of athletes dashing in and out of each other's rooms during the three Olympics I attended. Take hundreds of relatively attractive athletes in perfect physical condition from all over the world who have been living like hermits for four years, put them all in close proximity with each other and what do you expect? It's like a simple GCSE chemistry experiment, if you add certain basic elements into a confined cylinder under the right settings, intense reactions will happen.

We'd dissect potential love matches between athletes of different nations with the same intensity that we'd discuss our tactics in the relays. It was the perfect way to turn down the pressure and laugh.

One day I was walking through the Olympic village, down a quiet street, with my teammate Sarah Claxton, the 100 metres hurdler, when we saw two familiar figures. The late, great, Los Angeles Lakers basketball star, Kobe Bryant and his USA teammate Lebron James. From a young age, I was a dedicated Kobe fan and I was stunned. The USA basketball team were so popular amongst the athletes that they stayed in a hotel outside the village, but most of them still hung out in the village occasionally, alongside stars like Lionel Messi, the Williams sisters, Usain Bolt and Cristiano Ronaldo, before they all got mobbed and had to sneak outside for respite.

For once, Lebron and Kobe were completely alone, and Sarah elbowed me in the ribs. "You're never going to get this chance again, say something Anyika!" She was right, I had to do something. This was 2008, so I had no phone camera on me, my bulky digital camera was in my bedroom and I was far too old to be asking for autographs. I decided to keep it cool and casual. "Hi guys, what's up," I said, as calmly as I could, as if we were all standing in the queue for the local chippy back home in Liverpool after a night out.

Lebron and Kobe turned around in slow motion and smiled at us, "Oh hey ladies." In 10 seconds flat, they were mobbed from all directions. Two giant men buried beneath German shot putters, Japanese fencers and Iranian wrestlers and their digital camera flashes.

The coach for the 4x100 team was Roger Walters, who tragically lost his battle with cancer only five years after the Games. Roger was an old-fashioned gentleman who had found success with the silver medal winning British women's 4x100 team in the 2006 European Championships. He had competed as a sprinter himself in the 1972 Olympic Games in Munich and had gained a good reputation as a technical coach.

Unfortunately, coaching the niche points of sprinting with a single athlete and being in charge of a relay team with the difficult decisions that come at an Olympics is a completely different job description. You are not necessarily charged with honing sprinting technique, although that is part of your brief, you are there to make the hard calls and be the leader of a complex team.

Roger was under pressure from the start in a team with

strong personalities and ideas. There were seven of us vying for four coveted spots at the Olympics: Laura Turner, Jeanette Kwakye, Montell Douglas, Emily Freeman, Emma Ania, Ashleigh Nelson and me. When it came to the team decision ahead of the first heat, the team called a meeting.

The girls told Laura that they didn't feel that she was in good enough shape to run, having been knocked out in the first round in the individual 100 metres and they wanted to go with me for at least the heats, and then, depending on performance and if we qualified, the team for the final would be selected.

Laura was obviously upset by this, but equally, she completely understood the rationale behind the team's decision. The team's feedback to Laura might seem cold, and even callous, but this is the world we operate in as professional athletes.

Our job is to win medals and we deal with brutally honest feedback every day of our lives. Roger surprised us by saying that he was going with the same team in the heats as in the finals and neither included me. I was stunned. I had travelled all the way to Beijing in the hope of competing on the highest stage and instead ended up sitting in the stadium.

I tried my best to persuade Roger to give me a fair chance to show what I could do in the heat, but he told me that the call was out of his hands and that's all there was to it. I am not proud of it, but I really laid into him and told him that he was making a seriously weak call. Roger was an extremely nice man, but ultimately, he was not a leader or able to make strong decisions when it mattered. In an Olympics, that is not good enough.

Ultimately, Roger didn't pick Laura, but went with a team of Jeanette, Montell, Emily and Emma. I watched the girls in the 4x100 final from the beautiful Bird's Nest stadium with Ashleigh, disappointed, but also excited for my teammates. There was never going to be a better opportunity to medal for GB in this relay and maybe even win gold. The USA team had been disqualified and only the Jamaican team, led by sprint legend Shelly-Ann Fraser-Pryce, who had already won the 100 metres, looked dominant.

In the end, it was one of the oddest Olympic relay finals the world had ever seen. On the second relay changeover, there was an issue with the baton changeover for both Great Britain and Jamaica and neither country managed to finish. Gold went to Belgium, not traditionally known as a sprinting powerhouse, with Nigeria taking silver and bronze going to Brazil.

When you are watching your teammates and friends race, you are completely helpless. You wonder if you would have done anything differently, but ultimately it is pointless thinking like this. I later found out that, during a kit check from the officials in the first call room, one of the girls had a bad panic attack, and started asking "Where are my spikes? Where the fuck are they? I can't find them."

Normally, you are wearing your trainers, and have your

spikes in a bag to save the pins away from the track. It turned out the spikes were on her feet the whole time. A teammate later told me that once that had happened, they knew that the race was over before it had begun.

You are dealing with such small margins in the Olympics. The slightest disadvantage, whether physical, such as the Jamaican changeover mishaps that disrupted the team, or mental, can play complete havoc with the race. The mind can be calm throughout the whole Olympic experience, and then, just when you need it to stay on an even keel, it starts short-circuiting. Four years of careful and unstinting preparation blown to pieces by a seemingly tiny thing. In the relay, it doesn't take much for the carefully placed dominoes to fall over.

After the race I walked down to see the girls in the warm down area. You never know what to say in these moments, so you try to bring any comfort you can, but you know that it's pointless. Their emotions were raw and wild. No hug or kind words will ever absolve the pain of a missed chance in the Olympic final. I was heartbroken for the girls.

I looked at their faces and saw that their minds were trying to compute what had happened, but they weren't able to come up with an adequate solution. I had never seen that level of sadness at a competition, and I knew that these women were going to replay this race for the rest of their lives.

I was dealing with my own complex emotions after the

final. I felt sad and disappointed for the girls, but I also felt jealous that I hadn't had the opportunity to compete in that Olympic final. Your mind starts to play out detailed fantasies, could you have been the difference and won that medal? You never will know. I feel guilty for even admitting this now, but it's true, I felt jealous. I wanted to be out there and I wanted to create history in Beijing, particularly with this team that had an amazing depth of talent and always seemed to get it right.

It wasn't just a missed opportunity for a medal, it represented a lifetime of work for everyone who competed.

The next day we had a meeting with Dave Collins, the Performance Director at British Athletics, and Roger. The tension in the room was crisp, and Roger was not the right man for the situation.

We needed him to shout and scream, to demand why we had been such a good team only to blow it when it really mattered. By doing this, he would have at least given a focus for the bubbling anger and resentment that was building in the room.

"I know you're all disappointed, and I share that feeling with you," Roger began, unsteadily. "Now is not the time for blame, we simply have to find answers, and I want to hear from each of you. I need your perspective on what happened out there."

He was met with silence. His gentlemanly manner would have been better suited chairing a parish council meeting in middle England, not an Olympic debrief. He continued to talk, saying a lot of words, but unfortunately never finding the right ones. His polite preamble slowly and inadvertently built the kindling for a fire that was about to explode.

Roger eventually found refuge in the large screen television that played the race in achingly detailed slow motion. The race would then be replayed again and again, from a different angle in high definition. We were watching a horror movie where every single movement and mistake is highlighted to your peers. I was confused.

Guilty that I felt relief that I hadn't been out there making the mistakes, but also still upset that these talented women hadn't been able to show the world how good they were.

Out of nowhere one of the girls spoke. "Let's be real here. We lost the race before we even started, we weren't in the right headspace, you're competing in an Olympic final and I see a teammate unable to find her spikes that are on her feet? She wasn't focused on the race and we all crumbled."

The tension in the room had violently popped. Tears started and people started shouting, demanding answers of each other, our coaches and the race that never came. Everyone was crying including me.

It slowly turned from a vicious blame game to consoling each other. We all wanted to see growth and success for this team. We had invested our lives in the success of this Olympic medal. We had fought to be taken seriously, demanding physios, psychologists and proper funding like our male counterparts, yet we had this chance to write our name into the history books and blew it.

It wasn't one person's fault, it was the cruelty of elite sport.

Every major championship provides lessons to learn for every athlete. Even though I hadn't competed on the track as an Olympian in Beijing, life would come full circle when I would return there to compete in the Bird's Nest in the World Championships in 2015.

Beijing provided a small taste of the Olympic experience, and I was desperate for a bigger portion. I had come close to putting my spikes on an Olympic track, but perhaps I had let complacency set in. London was hosting the Olympics in four years and the motivation of running in front of my family and friends drove me to new levels as an athlete.

Christine and I had been sharing a room throughout the Games and I was able to get a front row seat into what made an Olympic champion. Christine never really changed her preparation throughout the Games, she had everything scheduled down to the minute.

Whether it was reading in her room, or watching TV, it was written down in a diary. We'd laugh in the same way that we always had since we were young and it was great to be there with one of my best friends as she proved the world wrong.

On the day of her final she was completely relaxed, as if it was a normal day of training at Lee Valley Athletics Centre. Before my biggest races as an athlete, I was always taught that there's comfort in being busy, particularly with my hands.

On the day of a final, I would do crossword puzzles, colouring books, writing or drawing, like a particularly active pensioner in a nursing home. Christine didn't need as many distractions, often happily losing herself in a novel. Just before we left the apartment for the Olympic final, I looked at her and asked, "Do you trust yourself?" she smiled back and nodded. I then said, "Let's go and win that title."

My greatest pleasure of the Games was seeing Christine win gold in the 400 metres. The same chilled and happy girl I had met in the dormitory in France had dealt with all the brickbats from the tabloids and had won gold in the 2007 World Championships. People were quick to point out that in Osaka she hadn't had to face the great American runner Sanya Richards.

On her day, and particularly that Olympic year, Sanya was the quickest 400 metres runner in the world, but I knew that Christine had the strength to beat her.

Richards had one of the quickest starts in the 400 metres, almost like a yellow jersey in the Tour de France, trying to break away from the crowd early to build a dominating lead and break her competitors psychologically and physically. Christine always had a beautiful flowing running style that went well with her calm personality and I knew, in spite of Richards' strong lead going into the final straight, that Christine could catch her in the last 100.

Christine came from far behind to burn through her competitors in the final sprint of the 400, just when your legs are loudly screaming for mercy from the smouldering pain of the lactic acid. I sat in the stadium and screamed throughout the whole race.

I was delighted to see my closest friend in the sport win Olympic gold, but also to have had the strength to keep going when she dealt with every untrue accusation that came her way throughout her ban. Christine's Olympic gold was vindication for all of the unnecessary abuse that she had taken for far too long.

Christine managed to forget her podium tracksuit, which they always tell you to pack if you get to a final, almost like an actress with her pre-written Oscar speech tucked in their ballgown. I sprinted to get her tracksuit just in time and sneaked in to see her in the presentation area with her coach, the late Lloyd Cowan and Christine's brother.

I vividly remember that Sanya was standing alone, refusing to engage with anyone, later disclosing that she had decided to have an abortion two weeks before the Olympics, leaving her in serious distress.

Christine's triumph also made me question my own career and future as an athlete. I had lived in Liverpool my whole life and it was a home that I loved, full of comfort with my family and friendly faces.

Comfort can make you complacent and that is not a mindset that you want to get into as a professional athlete. I had already seen it in other competitors, who would do just enough every year to get funding, then happily slip back into third or even second gear and cruise through the left lane of life, never pushing themselves to new and uncomfortable places.

I wasn't raised like that, and I knew my life would have to change.

I spoke to Christine and she understood how much I loved Liverpool, but she asked me if I was really being pushed to my limits there in an elite environment. Morris was a brilliant coach and an even better man, but most of my teammates were club level athletes and I wanted to achieve things in the London Olympics.

With the encouragement of my Dad, I briefly considered moving to Sheffield to join up with Jess Ennis-Hill's coach, Toni Minichiello, but London was calling.

I decided to live with Christine and join her coaches, Lloyd and Christine Bowmaker, to take my sprinting to the next level in the capital.

11

London Calling

EVERYONE ARRIVES in London with a purpose, often to make something new out of their lives and I was no different.

At 24, I was coming into my expected peak years as an athlete and traded the life I loved in Liverpool for a challenging and uncomfortable one in the capital. I had been given a tiny taste of the Olympics and needed to go to London to push myself to the next level in my sport. I had relatives in London but was grateful to move into Christine's flat and at the start, life seemed to click together nicely.

I had two new coaches in Lloyd and Christine and travelled to Lee Valley Athletics Centre to join my new training group. The track at Wavertree was as familiar to me as a comfy old pair of trainers. I had been competing on it since I was a young girl, and maybe I had enjoyed the status of being one of the club's few Olympians. I moved to London to push myself to the limits and became a small fish in an unforgiving and often impersonal sea.

From my first sessions with Lloyd, I knew that my body was being pushed far harder than it had been before. I just wasn't conditioned to deal with this step up in training and I was in serious trouble physically. It was as if I had enjoyed a successful career with Tranmere Rovers as a local hero but was now training and competing with the superstars at Liverpool.

When you run for a living, you become extremely sensitive to the needs of every part of your body and you almost have an inbuilt pressure gauge that tells you when you're going too hard. In Lee Valley, my pressure gauge was pushing into the red zone every day and was on the verge of snapping.

I didn't blame Lloyd for pushing me so hard. It just justified what Christine Ohuruogu had been telling me for so many years. She was right, I was never going to get to the next level as an athlete if I had stayed in my comfortable routine in Liverpool, no matter how much I loved my coach and club there. I was slowly building a stronger conditioning base and while my mind was ready for it, my body couldn't handle it. I dealt with debilitating knee injuries, as my body broke down under the weight of the new training regime, mimicking Christine's daily workout, which had propelled her to Olympic gold.

I had moved into Christine's flat in Newham, but within six months, she had bought a bigger house and moved out. I don't believe you ever really know someone properly until you live with them, and that was certainly true with Christine.

My Hidden Race

The girl that I had bonded with over shared Nigerian family experiences had grown up into an Olympic and World Champion with everyone wanting a piece of her. The hallway of the flat was always covered in envelopes, filled with invites to events all over the UK, ranging from the Brit and GQ awards to seats at Wimbledon.

At times in London, we were like ships in the night, at other times I was happy to be her plus one for the Brits. We were always friendly and Christine was still great company, but that late-night laughter that we had once enjoyed when we were younger had become rarer as life got a lot busier for both of us.

In all my years in Liverpool, I had never really seriously dated anyone. Honestly, I never felt that I was desirable to men. It was never easy. Black men weren't interested in me, and white guys either didn't find me attractive, or if they did, they fetishised me as an object. I spent so many nights in nightclubs in Liverpool ignored as I stood to the side while my school friends were swarmed by male admirers. London was a completely different matter. On every street and every corner, I saw a broad mix of cultures and colours and I felt alive.

Whether I was on the Tube or working, I was regularly getting chatted up by men of every kind of background. I was dating white, black and Asian guys. For the first time I had felt attractive, and loved the confidence that it gave me. I had stepped into a new world.

Christine and I were ultimately leading two completely different lives in London. I was still dedicated to carefully honing my craft as an athlete, whereas Christine was a defending Olympic champion getting pulled in different directions by the demands of her new profile.

I was always grateful for Christine's kindness in offering me a roof over my head, and the push to take my career to the next level. Ultimately, I regret how I came and disrupted her life. Christine is organised and meticulous, and I came in and brought a level of chaos that was difficult for either of us to reconcile.

Our friendship was still there, but I noticed that at times I was inadvertently annoying her. My Toyota Yaris had finally broken down and I was without any transport for four months when I arrived in London. I was completely reliant on Christine for lifts from the flat in Newham to Lee Valley for training and I could tell that she was getting annoyed by this, but she would never tell me.

I learned to negotiate the Tube very quickly. We had always had an unbreakable bond off the track and I would have trusted Christine with my life, but our friendship had changed since I arrived in London. Some of the bonds that held us together for so many years had loosened ever so slightly. There was never an argument, or tension, merely an unspoken realisation that we were both getting pulled in different directions.

I lived in London for four years and if I had to come up

with one word to define my time there, it would be 'struggle'. The word 'struggle' instantly strikes most people as negative, and of course it can be, but it can also lead you to achieve things that you never thought possible. My experience is relatable for lots of adopted Londoners, regardless of what career you find yourself in. On some days the world is at your feet, on others this huge city has beaten you to the ground for another day. Although I had my small shoe contract, I struggled financially throughout my time in the capital, but equally, I pushed myself in ways I never thought possible, emerging as a far stronger athlete and woman. The safety blanket of Liverpool with my friends and family had been well and truly ripped off.

From my first day in London, I was hustling for jobs off the track. I was an Olympian, but thanks to a combination of injury and loss of form, at the end of 2010 I got an email to tell me that I was off funding. The news came on my birthday. I was 26, had a small amount saved in the bank, but had invested all my time and energy into becoming a professional athlete. I had little to show for it bar a mound of Olympic kit. I now begin to understand why the aunties in the Igbo Club were so quick to tell you how well their children had done in their accountancy exams. They weren't boasting about them winning the County 100 metres championship for good reason.

Funding can help you sink or swim as a British athlete. Unlike a lot of countries across the world, we are lucky enough to have some access to National Lottery funding that can propel the country's medal count at every Olympics. As an athlete, your funding is reviewed every year, with a variety of things taken into account, namely, are you likely to win a medal at a World Championships or an Olympics. If not, at the very least you need to be in contention to make a final for a major event.

On paper, getting funding is a fairly black and white decision. Have a look at the athlete's results, their form and make an informed decision. Unfortunately, like a lot of things in life, it is often more grey. Influential coaches can bend the ear of the decision-makers, so an athlete that hasn't delivered results can get a stay of execution and remain on funding.

An athlete who has grafted in the shadows and achieved the requisite results can be left sitting without funding indefinitely. It shouldn't happen, but unfortunately, sometimes it does.

If you're lucky enough to get funding, the money isn't huge. The millions that are made through marketing, media and tickets at the events rarely make their way to the athletes' bank accounts. For every Usain Bolt, there are thousands of Anyika Onuoras. If you're in contention to win a medal at an Olympics, you could be awarded just shy of thirty grand in funding. If you're a likely finalist in a major championship, you could get just over twenty thousand pounds in support.

The funding is vital as it also enables you to gain access to a pile of other things you will need to compete at the highest level, money for coaches, warm weather training, medical staff and access to the best facilities. I have also known athletes who are supporting their whole extended family on this funding. They are not just running for medals, but to keep food on their family's plate.

Once you are out of that funding cycle, life as a professional athlete becomes all about survival, especially if you're living in London. It's a catch 22 situation, you need the funding to access the programmes that allow you to stay on funding. Without funding, you are not only financially in the red, but also constantly terrified of getting injured. One bad injury, without the necessary medical assistance that a funding programme brings and your career could be over.

Outside of funding, you are wrestling in the murky world of shoe contracts. I had signed with a sports company in 2005 and alongside a very small retainer, I was given as much training kit as I could carry.

Where most athletes make their money is through a bonus system that most sports brands operate, dependent on your place on the podium. If you are lucky enough to be considered attractive in the eyes of the British mainstream media, you might find that the brand uses your image in their adverts, nudging your pay that bit higher.

Ahead of each season, whether I was on funding or not, I would look at my finances and crunch the numbers. My degree in economics had made me relatively competent with an Excel spreadsheet and I was able to work out the gaps in the year. I would then spend part of the year handwriting and typing letters to companies across Liverpool, seeking sponsorship for major events to make up any shortfall in funding.

Some athletes thrive on this innovative approach and Louise Hazel, a gold medallist in the 2010 Commonwealth Games in the heptathlon, drove a campaign where she secured 12 local sponsors to drive her funding for the London Olympics. James Ellington also auctioned the opportunity to sponsor him for 2012 on eBay, before eventually securing significant backing from the King of Shaves company after the winning bidder backed out. In athletics, the graft often doesn't just finish when you take off your spikes, sometimes it has only just begun.

In London, you have to work hard to survive, no matter what career you choose. You look at any street in the city and people are hustling. Whether it's the man twirling the Golf Sale sign on Oxford Street, or businesswoman rushing off the Tube for another meeting, people are in perpetual motion. Most people who arrive in London come with a purpose in mind. Dick Whittington came to find streets paved with gold, I came to become one of the world's best athletes and both of us ended up disappointed.

From my first day in London, I knew that I had to find a job fast. When I wasn't training with Lloyd, I was out doing any kind of work possible. Recently, I counted that I had a total of 12 jobs outside athletics during my time in London. I filled temporary office jobs, served canapes at corporate events, I babysat, froze through a long winter as a leaflet distributor and I did telesales.

For any prospective telemarketer, I would advise you to learn a Scouse accent fast, and preferably, a female one. It worked wonders for me. I would never say that my name was Anyika. I'd choose something easy like Debbie or Sarah. After a bit of banter and patter, it wasn't long before I had the customer switching over to a new broadband provider. I was a regular on the top of the telesales podium.

However, I knew I wasn't going to join the Wolf of Wall Street anytime soon and applied for another office job with a construction firm. The owner didn't hire me for my administrative skills, but when he had a good look down my CV, he asked me if I was interested in coaching his son. I wondered if he was an athlete, he replied, no, his son was going to be the future of Chelsea Football Club. Regardless of whether the child would ever play at Stamford Bridge, I enjoyed my weekly visits to the mansion to teach little Archie how to get his strides correct.

I also had a regular gig serving at corporate events in the City of London. Between serving nibbles and drinks, I'd regularly see the great and the good of all sections of English society do drugs and drink long into the night. Regularly, the patrons of these events would invite me to a local BDSM club, where they would continue the party and be happily punished by a dominatrix. A law firm's CEO who had invited me introduced me to his friend who quickly looked me up and down like a car in a dealership and said "yeah, she's perfect, exactly what we're looking for tonight." I politely declined.

Like most adopted Londoners, I treated my bank account like a school report card. I didn't want to look at it too closely if I could avoid it. I was travelling home from training one day on the train chatting to a close friend. I was speaking quietly, but it was one of those days in London where nothing is going right. I told her I was going through it mentally, physically and financially. My athletics career hadn't turned out how I had planned. I couldn't even return to Liverpool, as I didn't want to come back a failure.

When I hung up the phone, a nice lady sitting opposite me introduced herself. "Hi love, I'm sorry to do this, but I couldn't help but hear your conversation," she said. "I just wanted to check you're all right?" In London, the kindness of a stranger is something to be cherished. I told her that I was all right, but yes, things had been a bit tough recently. I was always trying to clear my overdraft, but no matter how many jobs I had off the track, I just couldn't seem to win.

The lady was patient and listened to me. She told me that she had heard my accent and thought that maybe she had a job opportunity for me. "Sales?" I asked, suddenly interested. "I've actually done quite a bit of that, so I might be interested." The lady said that it was more customer service that catered broadly to male demographic. Naively, I asked where were the women customers? She eventually told me that she ran a telephone sex service and, with my accent, the rate started at £80 an hour rising to £250 an hour.

Can you honestly imagine a Christian woman raised in a strict Nigerian family talking dirty to old men? I didn't think that I fitted the job description, but this lady had definitely got me intrigued. I needed to pay for winter training, medical bills and my rent. I could do this job from my armchair reading a book.

She asked me if I wanted to see a sample script that some of her girls would use for customers. After twenty seconds, I had read some incredibly perverted prose and must have looked visibly shaken, as she told me lots of girls were shocked at the start, but they got used to it.

She asked me to take her business card and I did. I left it by the side of my bed for a week, not sure whether to call the lady. Eighty quid to sit at home and read a piece of paper? I wouldn't even need to see the people I was talking to.

Ultimately, I knew I couldn't do it, regardless of how much I needed the money. I wouldn't have lived to tell the tale with my Mum and Dad. I just didn't throw the business card in the bin, I burnt it, so there was no temptation to apply when my monthly bank statement came in the post.

After dealing with injuries throughout 2009, in 2010, my body broke down completely and I wasn't able to compete due to a bad quad injury. My bodyweight fluctuated wildly, and I began to put on unwanted kilograms. I remember meeting the head coach of UK Athletics, Charles Van

Commenee while I was working hard on an exercise bike at Lee Valley. Speaking to Charles, I thought that it was rude if I kept talking while cycling, so I went to get off. "Stay on," he said. "You look as if you need to."

In the tradition of many of his Dutch compatriots, Charles was not a man who believed in tact. He was direct and unable to make small talk. If he had a point to make, you would have to hear it without any polite preamble to cushion the blow.

Sometimes Charles' chosen mode of communication would reach the wrong person at the wrong time. Once, during warm weather training, Charles and Lloyd had a difference of opinion during one of my sessions and almost came to blows. I yelled at both of them for ruining my session and like ashen-faced schoolboys with their heads bowed, they apologised and promised that it wouldn't happen again.

I was on a strict diet throughout my injury in 2010, which included only having water when I woke up and exercising furiously before I was allowed to eat breakfast. I would then only eat a small number of calories throughout the day. The diet plan wasn't designed for my body, which was strong and needed more fuel to be at its best.

I was also doing a lot of distance running work to burn calories that was ultimately taking away from my power and speed sessions later in the day where I would arrive feeling completely flat and exhausted. The plan wasn't good for me either physically or mentally.

I also didn't help myself by going warm weather training in Los Angeles and discovering a new found love in Auntie Anne's Pretzels. It's fine to have as a cheat snack once a week if you are burning off the requisite amount of calories, but I certainly wasn't while injured. It felt like I was in a fat club for athletes and I was the only paid up member.

Ultimately, my career was saved by the generosity of two medical practitioners who treated me for free. Unfortunately, I was taken off funding in November 2010 but despite this, these two men refused to stop treating me, even though I was unable to pay for their treatment as I was out of the system.

They simply believed in my potential and wanted to help, even if it had no direct benefit to their careers. They understood how difficult it was to compete while off funding and juggling other jobs in London and they did everything in their power to get me back to my best.

Glenn Kearney was a Kiwi nutritionist who worked with the All Blacks and went on to help Andy Murray with his diet. His impact on my life was immediate. Glenn was one of the first nutritionists to consider an athlete's cultural background, be it African, Polynesian, European or Asian. He would then go through the foods we had grown up eating, were used to eating and liked eating.

He would then extrapolate how much of this food was needed for your chosen sport and what to avoid. I love Nigerian food, but a lot of the dishes are filled with starch, and not helpful for a track athlete if that's all you eat, so he helped me widen my culinary outlook, while still allowing me to have jollof rice once a week as a treat. Dr Gerry Ramogida worked during the week with athletes at Lee Valley, and at the weekend flew to be the physical therapist for the NFL's Seattle Seahawks. I have never met a man with a more hectic schedule, yet he still would insist on seeing me, for free, every Monday at 10.30am, shortly after touching down in Heathrow. Dr Gerry fought UK Athletics to treat me, as he knew I absolutely needed his help to come back from injury.

Gerry went on to achieve great success with the NBA championship winning team, the Golden State Warriors, and it's no coincidence that both he and Glenn went on to bigger and better things after UK Athletics. They helped me when there was absolutely nothing in it for them financially, or even reputationally, they just helped me because they wanted to see me succeed. I will be forever grateful for their kindness and sacrifice.

In 2011, after the difficulties of my early years in London, I had found a rhythm of sorts in the city. Due in large part to the sacrifice of friends like Gerry and Glenn, I had fought back to form. I ran a career personal best in the 100 metres of 11.18 in Zeulenroda Meeting in Germany. I was ranked first in the UK in the 200 metres after winning the British Championships, and second in the 100 metres. I felt that finally, I was going to get back onto funding and turbocharge my push for the Olympics in the city I now called home. Unfortunately, for reasons still not clear to me and in spite of my strong form, I missed out on funding once again. I didn't know how I was going to survive any longer living this life.

I had a fairly steady job doing corporate events for Newham Council, serving drinks and nibbles at various functions. It was tiring work, often I would be on my feet until late at night, knowing that in the morning I had to be ready to try and push myself to smash out sessions against full-time athletes. After one event, I was going home on a dark cold night and asked myself a question out loud that had been in my mind for a long time, but I had never actually spoken aloud.

"What the hell am I doing? Seriously, what kind of life is this? It's miserable, I'm exhausted and I can't go on doing this."

I said to nobody in particular. I sat on a bus stop alone in Newham on a freezing night at midnight and cried. I cried because in that moment my life felt helpless and pointless. I cried because I wondered was an athletics career seriously worth it? All this physical and mental pain to make the Olympic team while constantly struggling financially. I would be in the small print at the back of a newspaper if I was lucky. That would be my legacy of sacrifice and dedication to my sport. I had friends from university now happily paying off their mortgages and well into successful careers. London finally had me at breaking point.

It was one year before the London Olympics and I decided to keep going. I am still not quite sure why.

12

The Hope That Can Kill You

WHEN WE think of London 2012, most people think of grinning volunteers, packed stadiums, Super Saturday and endless British gold medals that came from the velodrome, the water and the track. The London Olympics and Paralympics delivered some of the greatest sporting spectacles the world has ever seen.

I only wish that I had been able to appreciate it fully.

After years of struggle in London – physically, mentally and financially – I had beaten the odds and made it to the Games, competing in the 100 and 200 metres individually. I had always had London in my mind, not only to prove to myself how far I had come, but to have my beloved Dad in the crowd.

Dad had been in and out of hospital for years and his health was deteriorating as he got older. I was getting used to phone calls from my family telling me that he had stopped breathing and I would speed up the motorway back to Liverpool.

Anytime I could, I would rush back to his bedside and he would softly chide me for missing training. I'd hold his hand and we'd talk about Liverpool FC, the Olympics and our bizarre shared love of a reality television show called *Cheaters*. We'd both happily sit together and watch this show where unfaithful partners would be exposed. Coming from his strict Nigerian family values, Dad just couldn't understand how people could destroy their families, and, like a car crash, he couldn't look away from this trashy show and I happily joined him.

On 2nd January 2012 I saw Dad for the last time. I knew that he was getting increasingly ill and I was desperate for him to survive until the Olympics. So many years ago, in that little Liverpool living room, it had been a dream, forged together while watching Denise Lewis winning gold in the 2000 Games. I was training hard for the Olympics and wanted to get back to see him, but my family told me not to, he wanted me to compete in London so badly.

Eventually, the phone calls with my family took a sharp turn, and I was told that Dad had days to live. The beloved man who had sacrificed so much to give me the life that I had, was lying ill in Liverpool, while I was miles away feeling utterly helpless.

I wanted to go back home immediately, but my family

told me to stay in London and they'd let me know when there was news.

I was wracked with worry, but as ever, the track remained my refuge and provided solace. When you feel at your most anxious, hard work acts as therapy, but as soon as I'd unlace my running spikes, the fear of Dad slipping away would hit me. I didn't want to look at my phone, because I knew that inevitably soon it was going to have bad news.

I was also working long shifts at the Royal Society of Medicine on their corporate events to keep my mind at peace. I was willing to work as long into the night as they wanted me to; anything to stave off the terror that my Dad was slowly leaving this life.

I started a shift at work at 10am and instantly felt relief when I had to put my phone in my locker. It meant that I didn't need to deal with the impending news about Dad that would cut me in half when it came. I was busy with another crazy day of ferrying plates and coffees across the function hall when a wave of emotion suddenly hit me. I had a strong feeling that the worst had happened, I just didn't know yet.

The clock nearly hit 6pm, and I begged my manager to work longer to delay the inevitable, but he said no, please go home.

I collected my phone from my locker and saw 176 missed calls. I stood in the middle of Oxford Street, one of the busiest streets in the world, feeling completely lost and panicked. I eventually composed myself and got onto the Tube, travelling from Bond Street to Canning Town, a journey that normally took around 30 minutes. There was no phone signal underground, and I told myself that Dad was still alive.

I wanted to slow down time and keep him with me longer. I wasn't ready to let go, not here on this train in London, alone. I hadn't picked up the phone to confirm the news, so I let myself believe that the man I adored most in the world was still there, ready to receive a phone call from me.

I thought about what we would speak about. Maybe we would complain about Liverpool's tactics in the league, or maybe I'd just tell him how that day's shift at work had been and how I was feeling about the upcoming Olympics. We spoke regularly, and Dad was always there to gently guide and comfort me, no matter how tough the world could be.

When the train pulled into Canning Town, I felt his tender grip on me loosen. I knew that I was going to have to confront reality as soon as I emerged from the underground onto my final journey home.

The 10-minute journey from Canning Town to Beckton on the Docklands Light Railway was when I knew I had to pick up my phone and speak to my family. I thought carefully about who I wanted to deliver the news to me. Maybe it was the athlete in me, but I desperately needed structure at that moment.

There were heavy tears forming, that would not stop

when they came, and I needed the news delivered clearly and concisely. I chose my brother Chiz Junior for that reason.

He had once saved my life as a young girl, and now he was going to be there as an adult to deliver information that I never wanted to hear.

"You alright kid?" he started. I replied that I was coming home from work and was ok. We both danced around small talk that neither of us had any appetite for. He eventually broke the ice. "Listen, I've got some sad news, Dad passed away." There was a silence. "Are you ok?," he asked. I told him that I was fine, but asked did Dad have any pain? "No, no, he went peacefully. He just slipped away." He stayed with me until the train arrived at my destination.

The tension and hurt of losing my Dad suddenly exploded on a packed commuter train with the phone closely pressed to my ear. My eyes were bloodshot and tears fell furiously. A kind woman beside me gently mouthed, "Are you ok?". I nodded, so grateful for the kindness of that stranger, but also knowing that I was unable to tell her that I was broken emotionally, that the person I loved most in the world had left me forever.

I walked out of the station into the dark night, sidelined by Londoners huddled into their coats with their own worries. I was near Christine's house and rang her. She knew immediately what was wrong and told me to come straight over. She opened the door and gave me a tight hug. She hated to see me in this amount of pain. The girl she had known for so many years, who hated to make any kind of a fuss, just lay limp in her arms. Once again, Christine was there when I needed her, a sister to care for me. Lying in bed that night, I felt excruciating pain. I knew that Dad had left this life, and I was never going to see him again. I had lost my guiding light and I wondered would I ever feel joy again.

I returned home to Liverpool the next day to be with my family and stayed for five days, but the house was too full of his memories. I'd go into the living room and stare at his favourite chair where he'd watched the Olympics and Liverpool games with me.

Unwittingly, from that seat, Dad had managed to ignite a fire in me that had never been extinguished. In the weeks after his passing, I threw myself into work and track sessions, using my exhaustion as a coping mechanism. I rarely allowed myself to cry, as I knew that once I started, the pain of his passing would completely overwhelm me.

We had the memorial service at the family church in Mossley Hill and all the family wore traditional clothing. When I walked into the church, I was hit with a wave of sadness that sent a shiver down my spine. It felt like I had lost control of my body. I couldn't stop crying and I was in physical pain.

After the service, I sprinted to the car, where Bisi comforted me softly. Eventually, she told me we had company. Through puffy eyes, I looked in the car mirror and saw all of my school friends coming over. Just as those girls had protected me through the torment of teenage years, they continued to hold me close as an adult.

Dad died in February 2012, months before he would have seen his daughter cheered loudly by a packed London stadium when they announced her name. He died of pneumonia and, in the hospital, the extended family had finally united.

After all those late-night Olympic telly marathons with Dad, I wondered just how much his chest would swell when he saw his daughter at the starting blocks in her GB kit. He was always proud of me, as I was of him. His sacrifices as a migrant had given me the platform to get to those Games, and I was determined to honour him.

In May, I was invited to travel to Brazil to compete for a series of lucrative meetings that would allow me to make some quick guaranteed cash. The races were in Belem, Fortaleza, Uberlandia and finishing in the heaving metropolis of São Paulo. The lure of a healthier bank balance was always tempting; but I never should have gone into such unchartered territory in my mental state. I was still emotionally raw from losing my Dad and would sometimes find myself automatically dialling his number to have a chat, and then remembering that it was too late. He was gone forever.

I arrived in Brazil stalked by a seething grief that wouldn't leave me alone. Thousands of miles from home it followed me to the track, through the unfamiliar streets and back home to the hotel where I spent each night alone. I didn't know a single athlete there, and have never felt so lonely, before or since. I had nobody to talk to and sat helpless in a mess of my own making. I crossed off the days until I could return home, as I completed a whistle stop tour of a country that I was unable to appreciate. It was the longest two weeks I ever spent as an athlete.

By 2012, I had been travelling around the world for years as a professional athlete, competing in some of the world's most amazing stadiums, but nothing will beat the noise and fervour that came in London. You would get off a bus in your team tracksuit and get mobbed for selfies. I was delighted that Anyika Onuora from Liverpool was starting to get a little fan club, when I heard somebody yelling, "Christine, Christine, can we please get a picture?". Even though there is no real physical resemblance between Christine Ohuruogu and me, that didn't stop me getting recognised as the defending 400 metres Olympic champion everywhere.

At the Olympics, you want to ensure that you have got the best possible roommate. Luckily, I had developed more experience as an international athlete and, as I got to know more people on the circuit, I was eternally grateful I didn't have to share rooms with any more naked German shot putters. In London, where once I would have shared with Christine, I shared with another 400 metre hurdler, Perri Shakes-Drayton.

Perri was the perfect person to have by my side in London, a sunbeam of positive energy that I badly needed after losing my Dad. In the intense atmosphere of the Games, Perri was there to take your mind off the pressure cooker of competition and laugh loudly.

You had the whole of Britain hooked up to the Olympics and my phone had to be left in a dark room to recover, it was vibrating with so many ticket requests from family and friends. Perri's fun personality was the perfect pressure gauge in an Olympic village that was pulsing with energy and expectation.

I could not have had two more different personalities for a coaching team. Christine Bowmaker was a former British athlete and brought a considerable contrast to Lloyd Cowan's relaxed Jamaican vibe. Christine didn't do anything without intensity, even something like eating her breakfast would have a planned purpose and timeline.

During the Olympics, in the middle of the most intense pressure, Lloyd could be found laughing and joking with old friends from the Jamaican set-up. His jovial nature could soothe the most searing nerves. Together, when it worked, they provided me with what I needed to compete at my very best. My ying and yang coaching team.

At this stage in my career, I was still a specialist sprinter. After a few days of soaking in the vibe of the Olympic village, it was time to compete in heat two of the 100 metres. The heat was on a Friday, one day before Jess Ennis-Hill, Greg Rutherford and Mo Farah won gold on arguably the greatest night in British Athletics. I always found the 100 metres a fascinating event in the Olympics. It happens in seconds, but it captivates the crowd like no other event. In a way, it defines the modern Olympics.

I entered the warmup track and went looking for Lloyd. I needed a coach's reassurance and some quick trigger words to get me focused. Lloyd was nowhere to be found. He had got the wrong bus and hadn't got to the stadium on time.

I made my way to the first call room, filled with aggressive sprinters staring each other out. We were told to go to the second call room and had to walk 400 metres up a small, steep hill, not the best preparation before the biggest race of your life.

I finally walked out into the Olympic Stadium, and when my name was announced, Anyika Onuora, representing Great Britain and Northern Ireland, I heard a deafening roar from the whole stadium. I saw the British flags waving when my name was called and thought of how proud Dad would have been.

Could he have imagined this in his wildest dreams when he first arrived to work on the docks in Glasgow? Teammates had talked about this Olympics being like nothing they had experienced before, and preparing for my heat, I understood exactly what they meant.

I told myself to breathe, to remember all of the sacrifices I had gone through in the last four years. Not knowing how I was going to fill my car with petrol, hustling for work and somehow still competing at the elite level to get here. I had finally arrived where I was meant to be. I said my prayer and got into the blocks.

You can do four years of intense preparation, do everything correctly and still fail badly. People do it every day for their university exams. It all comes down to one moment and you hope that everything goes well. The biggest exam of my life happened in front of a packed Olympic stadium, with friends, family and acquaintances expecting me to blow the competition out of the water. This exam would take just over 11 seconds, and I knew that I was absolutely capable of qualifying with relative ease when I looked around at my competitors.

The gun goes. I know I am an average starter, so I tell myself not to panic. There are bodies rushing past me, but I still have a strong finish in me as always. I push harder for the last 60 metres at full acceleration.

My body is in full flow, but somehow, my muscles do not seem as loose or as compliant as normal. I cross the line and it's over for me in 11.41 seconds, far short of my personal best of 11.18. Like the maths test at school, where you know that you've missed a few difficult questions that you revised, but still hope your overall paper has got you that coveted grade. I waited. I looked up at the scoreboard, I had finished fifth. There's no way that I will be able to qualify for the semi-final. I don't understand what's gone wrong, I had done everything right, but when the starting gun went, I simply didn't perform on the biggest stage.

I walk down the stadium corridor in disbelief. I am too stunned to process any logical thoughts. A Papua New Guinean athlete jogs up and tells me she was so honoured to compete with me. I thank her. "I never thought in my life that I would run against a defending Olympic champion, thank you, Christine," she said. I am too shocked to reply.

Four years of living on the edge in London to compete like that? I see Karen Forbes, the UK Athletics competitions coordinator. Karen is the kind voice that you need in a crisis. "You'll be ok Anyika," she said. "You can definitely still qualify." I wish I shared her optimism, and after watching the next heats come through, it's confirmed, I am out of the Olympic 100 metres.

On television, on social media and in newspapers, we triumphantly celebrate our British Olympic champions and why not? They have achieved every child's dream by winning gold when the world is watching; but we rarely think of the hundreds of athletes every Olympic cycle, who have given up everything to compete and are knocked out in a few seconds. I certainly never thought of these athletes when I was cheering on Denise Lewis in Sydney with Dad. Why would I? Without realising it, or intending it, I had become a part of that huge faceless group of athletes. An Olympian in name, but quickly knocked out in the heat. I drop to the floor and tears run down my face.

I hear the roar of the crowd for my teammate Margaret Adeoye who has booked her spot in the semi-finals with a brilliant run. My emotions are twisted. I am happy for Margaret, but her well deserved cheers contrast with the silence that surrounds me. I feel like a failure and I can't speak. I walk around in a trance, before making my way to the kit collection. Karen is a veteran of numerous Olympics Games, and has seen the full spectrum of emotions of athletes. She slowly comes up and puts a tender hand on my elbow.

"Anyika, you'll be ok, trust me. It might not feel like it now, but you will get through this. Look at me, if you need me I'm here ok? Just go and get your stuff, and I promise you, you will be ok."

I want to sink into her shoulders and cry for hours. Instead, I join the queue to collect my kit in a daze. Once I have my stuff, I see Olympic teammates on their way to compete. They are focused, but also filled with positive energy. The possibilities are endless for them. Some hadn't seen the race, and assumed that I'd gone straight through to the semis. "Great job out there Anyika!" I hear someone say cheerily. I can't even look at them through my puffy eyes. I had to take a long walk to get out of the stadium that never seems to end. It feels like something in Alice in Wonderland, you are walking and can see the light, but you aren't making any progress. You are getting further and further away from where you want to go.

The next day I travelled to the relative calm of Lee Valley to meet my coach Christine, to work through where I had gone wrong on Friday. Christine worked on getting me to remember my steps and most importantly, to relax. I was lucky, I had another chance to try and make everything right in the 200 metres.

I channelled all of my communication via my brother Chiz Junior, as it was getting overwhelming. Vague acquaintances I hadn't heard from for years were asking for tickets to events and after parties. Where had they been a year ago when I couldn't get a sponsor and was crying at the bus stop after working with Newham Council?

I woke up on Monday in the Olympic Village and screamed. I was in agony from period pain which had stalked me sporadically ever since my Dad's death in February. My cycles were completely off, and when I needed it least, I would be crouched over in pain. I went to the doctors, but they couldn't give me anything stronger than Ibuprofen which did little to quell the agony.

I walked out to compete in heat two again, this time in the 200 metres. Allyson Felix, the brilliant American sprinter who went on to win gold in the Games, was in my heat.

Once again, my name was announced and there was a wall of sound from a packed stadium. I tried to take the moment in slowly. I made sure to smile at the volunteers collecting the kit, and to thank them before I stood at the blocks.

I looked around at the waving British flags and the flashes of light in the crowd. I had dreamt of this moment since

I was a little girl in Wavertree and I was representing my country in the London Olympics.

The 200 metres was the event where I always felt most comfortable. My relatively slow start could be compensated by a strong finish that, on my day, could pull back most competitors in the world. The gun went and I felt I was running well, except that the runners flying past me in my peripheral vision told me I wasn't. I rounded the final turn, held my breath for what we call the sling shot and braced myself for the final push down the last 100 metres of the track.

I increased my acceleration, but my legs felt like they were running through thick mud and my cadence was all wrong. My legs were not doing what my brain was commanding them to perform. An elite 200 metres event is over in just under 22 seconds, but this one felt like minutes. I had a high sensory moment, where I knew something was going very badly wrong, but I was utterly helpless to stop it. I felt more bodies fly past, and no matter how hard I tried to control the race, I was completely powerless. I crossed the line in fourth place in 23.23 seconds and shouted, "Fuck". I seldom swear. My Olympic Games were over, just like that. My heart was broken.

I want to leave the stadium as quickly as possible, but there is a crowded press gauntlet to walk through. Television cameras, national newspapers, even the *Liverpool Echo*, are wanting a quote. Pain and devastation can still sell a headline on a quiet day. I am too devastated to speak and I walk past on dead legs, hearing a chorus of angry journalists, before they move on to the next athlete in the media feeding frenzy. I am already yesterday's news.

I catch up with Lloyd, he berates me for my performance and I don't blame him. I am almost enjoying this bollocking because he is saying exactly what I think, except he's probably holding back a bit. Then suddenly it all becomes too much and I burst into tears. I hate crying in front of people, but I let myself do it here. I am powerless to stop it. All Lloyd can do is hold me close and tell me that somehow everything will be all right.

I arrive back at the Olympic Village and see that Perri isn't at home. If there was ever a time that I needed Perri's beaming smile and reassurance, it is now. I climb into the shower and start crying stinging tears. When you are a professional athlete, the shower is often the best place to cry and you quickly learn to do it there. You won't disturb your roommate and nobody needs to know the pain you are in as they almost certainly don't care. I cry for the wasted years of my adult life and I cry because all I really want right now is a hug from my Dad.

Eventually I stumble out of the shower, and another teammate, Marilyn Okoro, persuades me to come to the food hall with her. If nothing else, the people watching will provide us with the best couple of hours of reality entertainment possible. After speaking about everything apart from our athletics careers, Marilyn notices the UK Athletics head coach, Charles van Commenee, approaching our table and whispers, "I think he wants to speak to you".

Charles' Dutch directness is not what I ordered. "I suppose you've come to bollock me?" I ask. "No," he says, almost affronted. "I came to see if you were all right. Can you explain what happened?" I said that I was emotionally and physically drained and it just didn't click on the track. I didn't want to talk about how much I missed my Dad. There wasn't the opportunity to talk about grief, everything was always about business. I didn't want to walk this man through my period cycles. I didn't want to tell him that to even get to the Olympics when you are pulling late-night waitressing shifts, flogging broadband packages and coaching kids on no funding, was a miracle.

He eventually leaves, but not before questioning whether pizza is a sensible food choice. I ignore him and eat another slice. Fuck him. Marilyn and I sit and talk until three in the morning.

I eventually go to sleep, but it is a fitful one. I toss and I turn and I think of how I let myself, my family and my country down when I needed to deliver most. I eventually fall into a deep sleep and wake up in the late morning hoping that my Olympic experience in London was a nightmare. I quickly realise when I pull back my Team GB bedspread that it is only too real. This was the one Olympics I needed to deliver in and I haven't done anything of the sort.

I had dedicated everything to this life and had been quickly knocked out in two heats.

I seek refuge in the shower once again and turn music up loud to provide some sort of distraction for my fractured mind. As the hot water hits me, the tears won't stop, but neither will the negative thoughts now piercing my brain. 'You gave up your life to compete like that in front of the world? You had your whole community and family watching and you ran like that? After everything you've been through, all that sacrifice, and you've blown your one shot here in London.'

I decide right there to kill myself. I have defined my life by this sport and have got nowhere with it. In the Igbo community, my mother and my aunties have been proudly telling everyone about Anyika the Olympian. Now that Olympian feels a complete fraud and failure.

I need to kill myself, but I am not sure how. I briefly think of hanging myself, but even in my despair, I am logical and know that no length of cloth will take my body weight. I just want it over and I become manic. I want to climb out of the window and fall from a height, but the window won't open fully. I start headbutting it with full strength. The piercing pain in my head almost feels good, as if I deserve to feel this way.

I turn to the bathroom; there are a set of scissors. They are sharp enough to cut open my wrist and I will bleed to death in the Olympic village. Short and swift. A forgotten

Olympian who was tired of making up the numbers for another year.

I have the scissors in my hand and am about to make the first crisp cut into the soft flesh when I faintly hear Perri, but I am facing away from her. She is trying to talk. I vaguely hear her. "Anyika? Anyika? Hello? Can you not hear me?" I do, but then again I don't. My mind eventually moves from the act of planning to kill myself, to engaging in conversation.

She turns me around gently with her hands. She sees me crying and envelopes me in a huge hug, telling me that I'll be ok. I slip the scissors up my sleeve as we hug. She doesn't see a thing and I agree to go down for food with her.

Eventually, I snap out of the mental storm and join Shana Bingham, Shara Proctor and Tiffany Porter in the casual dining area. They are chatting happily and I completely forget about the scissors which are still up my sleeve. How could I consider putting my Mum and my siblings through another death in the family? How can I let the London Olympics define my life in this way? *Is being an athlete all you stand for?* I feel physically and mentally drained. *My friends and teammates have no clue that, 10 minutes ago, I very nearly killed myself.*

I sit at the table eating a pastry, not realising that it has nuts in it which I am seriously allergic to. I start to have a bad reaction and the girls rush me to the Team GB medical room where the doctor goes to give me an adrenaline shot. He asks for my arm, instantly I remember that the scissors are up my right sleeve, and I offer him my left one. As soon as the doctor gives me the shot, I wait until he's not looking and throw the scissors over a cabinet out of sight.

A day after the Games, I decide that I want out of this sport. I am sitting in my apartment eating a commemorative block of Cadbury's chocolate given to every Team GB athlete with their name on it. The television is playing BBC's *The One Show*, which isn't exactly helping my depressive state.

The last pieces of chocolate are all I want to do with London 2012. I am just another athlete at the Games who crashed out of the heats, completely forgotten, apart from the microprint of dusty newspaper archives, that only the most avid athletics historian will ever find in years to come. I don't care whether I am known as an athlete anymore.

I want to start the next chapter of my life.

And I know that chapter does not involve running spikes and stopwatches.

13

Challenge Anyika

A MEETING with an American coach, Rana Reider, ultimately changed my destiny as an athlete completely. He was never an easy man to deal with, but I owe any success that came later in my career to his coaching.

After the disappointment of London 2012, I had told my boyfriend Rohan that I was ready to retire from athletics and start slowly climbing the corporate ladder. I had studied economics for enough years at university to understand that my return on investment in athletics was not enough to justify continuing. I looked forward to a life where I could switch off the computer at 5pm and not worry about my calorie intake that evening.

To say that Rana was a force of nature was an understatement. He had built a reputation as a world-class track coach, initially in the university circuit, with Kansas State and University of Florida. He would do anything for his athletes and would go anywhere in the world to support them, regardless of what it cost. He was obsessive about creating world-class athletes and joined UK Athletics in 2012 after the Olympics. Rana's designated brief was to oversee the sprints, sprint hurdles, horizontal jumps and sprint relay programmes. Not that any of this was relevant to me. I was more focused on finishing the Team GB stock of Cadburys' chocolate that I had been given in the aftermath of the Games.

Although Rana could change an athlete's life through his technical expertise, he would never win them over with charm and diplomacy. He was as subtle as a cold slap in the face. In the morning, without his sacrosanct double espresso, Rana was even blunter than usual. When we first met in Loughborough, Rana didn't try to sweet talk me with a slick sales pitch about continuing my athletics career – that wasn't his style. He was one of the best in the world in his field and he knew it. He laid out his cards and told me to take them or leave them.

"British athletes are lazy and soft," he began confidently. "There's nothing more a British athlete loves than sitting on their fat ass on the treatment table. I can make you into a world-class athlete Anyika, but I'm telling you it's not going to be easy. You're 27, so out of any athlete I'm willing to take on, you've got the biggest job ahead of you." Rana then rapidly began dissecting my weaknesses as an athlete, namely, my average starts out of the blocks and my diet. He was like a brusque surgeon, lacking any perceptible bedside manner, but it didn't matter, you would trust him with your life when it came to the operation and that is what matters ultimately. Rana began to win me over and slowly started to stitch my career back together.

Rana's genius as a coach was that he would strip you down like a high-performance machine, methodically analysing each part of what made you an athlete. He would carefully tweak aspects of your performance, but he would also leave the parts that he felt were working perfectly. If I had a tight achilles or calf muscle, he would be able to work on a holistic plan and adjust my training completely. He would do small, but significant, fine tuning to turn you into an athlete that would make the world finally stand up and take notice.

After the London Olympics, I moved to Loughborough to train full time with Rana in the Seb Coe High Performance Athletics Centre, otherwise known to all as HiPAC in autumn 2012.

Rana was coaching a core group that included fellow British athletes like Harry Aikines-Aryeetey, Tiffany Porter, Shara Proctor, Dwain Chambers, Martyn Rooney, Christian Malcolm, Chris Tomlinson and James Ellington. Rana also coached two US athletes, double Olympic gold medallist and World Champion triple jumper, Christian Taylor and the hurdler Danielle Carruthers, who had won silver in the 2011 World Championships. I instantly built strong friendships with Danielle and Christian, who brought some much-needed stateside glamour to suburban Leicestershire.

Rana coached me, but I was getting just as much benefit from being in a team environment filled with some of the world's best athletes. Danielle, originally from Kentucky, possessed cast-iron confidence, not only in her ability as an athlete, but as a woman. The first time I went into the weights room with her and started lifting my normal weights, she stopped me in my tracks.

"What the fuck is that?" she asked, looking shocked at my weights. "We out here chasing medals girl, so start lifting hard right now."

Danielle took me under her wing and provided a wall of strength in a turbulent world. She told me to stop giving a damn about how I looked and focus on becoming the best athlete possible. Danielle had been coached by Rana for years and also provided a perfect compass to navigate his unpredictable moods. She knew when to approach him and when to wait for the storm to pass. I followed her lead, on and off the track.

As you get older, close friendships often become that bit harder to form. When you are a professional athlete, it can become almost impossible. We are travelling throughout the year, briefly nodding to each other in the warmup area, before rushing to get to the next event. Like any workplace, there are people that you like and people you don't, and, like the office, when it's time to go home, you'd rather be with your nearest and dearest, rather than discussing your acceleration out of the final bend in the 200 metres.

In Loughborough, Rana's team of athletes became known by us all as the 'Tumbleweed Track Club'. We came from all over the place and we had no permanent home, hence the Tumbleweed moniker. Wherever Rana was, we followed. We never knew where we were going to end up, but we would always be together. On the track, it was business, and we drove each other to new levels of competition. Danielle and Christian brought their wisdom and knowledge from the American system and seamlessly blended into this group of British athletes.

Off the track, in a town mostly populated by students, we were inseparable. Most weekends, someone from Tumbleweed would host a BBQ or we'd all go out somewhere for dinner. In a cut-throat world, where athletes are not only fighting over results, but the next shoe contract, we had developed a global group of friends who would back each other completely. I would regularly hear Christian's loud American accent cheering for me from the long jump pit all over the world and it just bolstered our team spirit to new levels.

I needed the tight bond of Tumbleweed when I tried to rent a house in Loughborough. Many years had passed since my father struggled to buy a property in Liverpool due to the colour of his skin, and I was facing the same issues in the rental market three decades later. I visited an estate agent and was completely ignored, with a white lady behind me in the queue served before me. This lady pointed out to the estate agent that I was ahead of her and he then tried to serve me, but I was already walking out. When I finally got an appointment with an estate agent and was walking through an apartment, he told me that he would never rent an apartment to a Nigerian.

The British sprinter Harry Aikines-Aryeetey had kindly allowed me to stay at his house until I got settled, and his white housemate Olly kindly offered to help me get a place to stay. Olly joined me on my daily visit to the estate agent holding hands, with him acting as the dutiful boyfriend. The ruse worked perfectly, and I was soon renting a house in Loughborough. Loughborough is a town that moves to the rhythm of its vast student population, we all learned to sleep in tandem with the carnage from the loud and lairy drinking games in the streets below.

I was selected for the 2013 World Championships in Moscow, competing in the 200 metres and finished in an extremely slow time of 23.56 seconds. In spite of all the improvements that I had made as an athlete with Rana, I knew that something was badly wrong with my body in Russia. Before the championships, I had been in some of the best form of my life, becoming one of the few women who had run the World Championship qualifying times in the 100, 200 and 400 metres. I was fully expecting to be in the final and felt that my time had arrived.

In the first 200 metres of the heat, I was running with all of the confidence that my form justified and just as I went into the turn for the final 200 metres and about to really hit my stride, I felt the achilles go. People often talk about a mystery sniper shooting them when they suffer from severe hamstring tears. I definitely felt the sting of that sniper's bullet surge directly into my tendons during that heat, and, despite just about finishing the race, I knew that something seriously wasn't right.

I lay in agony in the kit collection room of the Luzhniki Stadium, unable to put any weight on my feet, only to be met by a drug tester asking to do a test. I knew that they were only doing their job, but I lost it. "Why the hell are you testing me?" I asked. "Did you not see how slow I was? Why the hell would I have taken performance-enhancing drugs running that time out there?"

I was even more angry to be tested because I suspected that the Ukrainian sprinter Mariya Ryemyen who won my heat was on performance enhancing drugs. Incidentally, she was caught a year later, serving just over two years. I eventually did the test, left the stadium on crutches with the team doctor Dr Rob Chakraverty and got an ultrasound back at the hotel.

Lying on my front, I scanned the medical team's faces for any clues and got none. They eventually told me that I had torn my plantaris muscle and it wasn't looking good. I was so delusional that I asked would I still be ok to compete in the relay and was told that my season was completely over.

I broke down in tears and Rana told everyone to get out

of the medical room. He gave me a big hug and told me that everything would be ok. He knew that it wasn't fair and he was just as cut up as me. Just when our carefully laid plan was ready to come to fruition, it was destroyed in an instant. I soon heard from my agent Caroline Feith. When you are lying helpless far from home with your career in the balance, you realise where you stand with your agent. I had seen many friends dropped like discarded supermarket receipts by their representatives after a bad injury. All Caroline cared about was my health. "If anyone can fight this Anyika, it's you," she said. "Whenever you need me you know that I'm here."

I waited in my hotel room in Moscow before I was allowed to fly home for surgery. I was visited not only by British teammates and friends, but also opponents from the United States and Canada who had seen the race, and wanted to see how I was. They told me that they had all been following my season and had seen how well I was running before the injury. At the worst of times, these small gestures of kindness from competitors across the world meant so much.

Surgery was gruesome and I have never felt pain like it before or since. They were unable to give me general anaesthetic because they were operating on my front, and if it was administered there was a chance I might not wake up from surgery. I was given local anaesthetic and I had no choice but to stay wide awake. I could feel the surgeon's scalpel scraping and carving all over my damaged plantaris muscle. I lay flat on my front for 45 minutes screaming. I nearly passed out from the piercing pain, but somehow stayed conscious throughout the operation. Every move from the surgeon was like getting stabbed in the leg with a coarse butcher's knife. Finally, it was over, and I lay crying on the operating table, swaddled in sweat.

When I was recuperating in the hospital post-surgery, I saw a familiar name flash up on my phone, the newly crowned World Champion, Christine Ohuruogu. Despite us growing apart, Christine was still the same person. She was ringing to check if I was all right and if there was anything she could do to help. Whether it was a recuperation team, or simply driving to the hospital to bring supplies, she was ready to do it.

At one of the lowest points in my career, Christine was again there when I needed her most. Asha Philip and her Mum, who I affectionately called Auntie Sharon sent flowers. I also got flowers and a beautiful note from Dina Asher-Smith who, at 18, was already showing the world that she was going to be an outstanding athlete, winning bronze in the 4x100 metre relay in Moscow.

I managed to get back on funding by the end of 2013, which promised a brighter future, but my body was held together by a thin thread. I had lived a life that thrived on routine and structure and now I was barely able to walk correctly. I fell into a deep, dark depression. All of a sudden, I was completely reliant on others.

In my life, I'd always wanted to do things myself, now

unable to drive, I needed help to even get to the supermarket.

In a university town, I was living a shabby student life, just without the academic requirements and promise of a brighter future. I was going to bed late, caught in a vortex of crap TV and a bad diet. I couldn't get around without a car, so I settled for greasy student-special pizza deliveries from Dominos. I was also drinking heavily, partly to numb the physical and mental pain that I was experiencing. I didn't know if my athletics career was ending, so I tried to find solace in the most useless place, a wine bottle.

I wasn't allowed to walk flat footed for my recovery exercises, so I had to wear heels on the steps. I would dress in my silk dressing gown and walk up and do my prescribed hourly calf raises on the bottom steps in my heels with a glass of wine in a rather pathetic and inadvertent tribute to Joanna Lumley's Patsy from *Absolutely Fabulous*.

I was alone in a dark home, unable to see my friends from Tumbleweed who were all away completing their seasons. I couldn't go anywhere, so I numbed my pain with cheap red wine. Drinking alcohol heavily when you're depressed is like trying to put out a fire with ethanol. It will cause even greater heartache and destruction. I would wake up late in the day with a pounding headache and often an empty bottle of wine would be by my bedside table. Was this the image I wanted to portray? To be honest, I didn't care at all.

I drifted into a dark place filled with disorder. One night I was watching TV until 2am, and I heard footsteps outside my house, just as I was getting out of my bed. I saw two guys trying to break into my car. My instant reaction was to run out and scare them, and then I realised that I was absolutely helpless. I couldn't move. I remembered that some of the boys from Tumbleweed would play with BB guns, and I grabbed one from under the bed. Like a sniper, I sat and fired off pellets at the intruder, and hit them a few times while screaming. Luckily they ran off, leaving me shaking with the rifle. Incidentally, my mother was staying the night with me, and slept blissfully through the whole ordeal in the spare bedroom.

Shara Proctor came over to my house unannounced one morning straight from the airport after winning the Diamond League final in Zurich and was shocked by what she saw. The Anyika she knew on the track was disciplined and utterly focused, now she was looking at a woman broken physically and mentally. She was banging on my door, but I wouldn't let her in, saying the house was a mess. Eventually I opened it, and she saw me dressed in heels, a dressing gown and a glass of wine.

My first words to her were damning. "Let's have a drink," I slurred. Shara ignored my invitation to drink a bottle of vinegary Chilean red, opened the curtains and made breakfast.

She instructed me to go into the shower and said that this behaviour couldn't continue. I was drinking my career away. Over breakfast, I agreed that I had to keep going and the drinking had to stop. I had faith that I could develop my career, I just needed one more night.

I went to a Tumbleweed BBQ that night, and told them to put on Kendrick Lamar's song *Swimming Pools*. The boys knew what was coming, and said no please don't do it. I said put on the song, and reluctantly they did. I sat and listened to the lyrics, while holding a bottle of 70% proof Jamaican rum:

> *I wave a few bottles, then I watch 'em all flock*
> *All the girls wanna play Baywatch*
> *I got a swimming pool full of liquor and they dive in it*
> *Pool full of liquor I'ma dive in it*
> *Pour up (Drank), head shot (Drank)*
> *Sit down (Drank), stand up (Drank)*
> *Pass out (Drank), wake up (Drank)*
> *Faded (Drank), faded (Drank)*

Every time Kendrick said the word 'drank', I complied, downing a shot of rum. I did this until the end of the song. I knew that was the end of my drinking days, and it was time to get my career back. The stitches from my leg were coming off the next day, and it was time for me to come back to what I loved.

Despite the disaster of the World Championships in Moscow in the 200 metres, an event in Gainesville, Florida, that had taken place months before, had given me hope that my career still had life in it. Tumbleweed travelled to Daytona Beach for warm-weather training and Rana asked me to compete in the 4x400 metre at the Florida relays. I was a pure sprinter and had no idea how to run this race. I told him I didn't want to do it, it looked too painful, but he didn't care. I kept hiding around the stadium, but Rana kept finding me. He often wanted his sprinters to do a 400 to build strength and endurance and now it was my turn.

I competed in Florida in an extremely quick international relay team with girls from Canada, USA and Britain, terrified that I would mess up, as I had no idea of how to pace the race. I somehow finished my leg in 52 seconds, relieved that I hadn't looked completely out of place. My time was good for a first timer, but my lungs were screaming for mercy and my legs were still burning with lactic acid. I had no intention of going near a 400 event again.

Rana had other ideas. He was convinced, with my strength, speed and power, that I was far better suited to this gut-wrenching sprint over a lap of the track. I hated the 400 metres, but if it helped me get better for the 200, then I was all for it.

After Florida, and just before the World Championships, I competed in two Diamond League events in Oslo and Monaco and I almost started to believe what Rana was saying. I won a meeting in Nancy, France, in 51.38 seconds from lane eight and felt a eureka moment.

I respond best to a challenge, and there was no greater

one than deciding to compete in a new event in your late twenties. I called it 'Challenge Anyika'. Over time I gradually left the explosive world of the sprints and moved into the tactical flow of the 400 metres. It was a significant gamble, but I didn't have many chips left on the table. I was still able to aim for the World Championships and Olympics in the 200 metres, but I wanted more. I wanted to win medals and so did Rana. If I was going to try to win a medal in the Olympics and not just be happy with a tracksuit, then there was seriously hard work ahead and I couldn't wait to get started.

Progress was slow as I started to develop my craft as a 400 metres athlete in 2014, but it was coming. I won two bronze medals, as part of the 4x100 and 400 relay teams in the Commonwealth Games in Glasgow. Both of these medals brought so much joy and really completely changed the trajectory of my career.

I always felt that I was forced to be a leader in the 100 metres relay teams that I competed in. If there was an issue with performance, or someone stepped out of line, I was the one that was asked to get the team into shape by the coaching staff.

I never questioned this role, and did as I was told, even if it meant that my own performance suffered. I was a 28-year-old fighting to compete against some of the fastest 21-year-old sprinters Britain had ever produced. The talent was so deep, that I was in a fight every day just to make the team.

Challenge Anyika

In Scotland, the England sprint coach Tony Hadley pulled me in for a meeting after the 4x100 heat. Tony is a man who doesn't need an excuse to get excited, and he was brimming with energy. "Anyika, we've got an idea. We want you to run in the final of the 400 metres relay instead of the 100. We've seen your speed, and we know that you can give us something different."

I wanted to be sick. Mentally I wasn't even sure if I could do it. I had been experimenting with the quarter mile with Rana, but not at this level. I knew the rhythms and routine of the sprint relays backwards, for the 400 metres I was barely sure where I was meant to stand. Tony read my mind, and looked me in the eyes. "You've got a packed house in Glasgow, and there is no better stage to show the world what you've got. We know that you're going to give us something special out there."

In the warm-up area of the final, I was mentally all over the place. I was stunned by Tony's faith in me, but still didn't think that he would select me in the final four runners for the final. I sat in the changing room at Hampden Park, the home of the Scottish football team, crippled by nerves. I was convinced that I would get the team disqualified due to a complete lack of knowledge of what I was doing.

I looked over at Christine, completely in her element, joking and laughing with Kelly Massey and Shana Cox. As usual, I felt a wave of calm and solace being near her.

I ran the final leg of the final, and after relative drizzle, the sky opened into a Scottish monsoon. I bounced on the spot, trying to stamp life into my legs and grip the surface with my spikes that had become almost as slippery as ice. I could barely see through the rain when I received the baton from Kelly. Jamaica and Nigeria were locked in a battle for gold and silver, and my first thought wasn't securing bronze, it was relief that the baton was safely locked in my grip.

The first two hundred metres of the race felt familiar, and I almost found myself enjoying it, being chased by a pack from behind led by Australia and Canada. The wind and rain were pounding my skin, and I could barely hear the raucous Scottish crowd that had made the Games one of the best ever.

I rounded the corner into the final 100 metres, fighting fatigue, thick rain and the fear that I was going to slip on weak legs. I started to over-compensate with my arms, pumping them to help drive my body through the final metres.

I didn't have the ability to turn my head to see if I had done enough as I crossed the line. My legs were burning, and it was almost an out of body experience for a split second.

Then I heard the roar of the crowd, the screams of Kelly, Shana and Christine as they jumped on me. I felt vindicated. I had doubted myself until I received the baton, and now I have shown the world that I might have what it takes as a quarter miler.

My life as an athlete changed forever on that rainy and happy night in Glasgow.

14

Assaulted

"ARE YOU following me up?" he said, laughing.

"No, I think you're following me up, lad," I responded.

I was in a lift heading up to my hotel room. It was near the end of a relatively successful season and I knew this sportsman, so it felt appropriate to exchange some innocent banter after we both pressed the lift button simultaneously.

I'd recently clocked my fastest time of the season and there was a lavish post-race banquet laid on that evening that was Gatsby-esque. No expense was spared on food and wine in a stunning location. The dinner was a relatively short drive away from where we were staying and I was heading back to my hotel room before heading out to get a bus to the venue.

My plan was to eat something and then return to the hotel as soon as possible. I was tired after a long year but was still doing my best to be social. It was a warm evening, and I was only drinking soft drinks to stay clear-headed before an early flight the next day. I also had a season to finish. The first bus back to the hotel was 9pm and I had just a few more hours of this event to go.

It was later on that evening that I saw the man I'd met in the lift. He was drinking a lot and clearly enjoying himself. I was nibbling on antipasti and chatting to other athletes, just enjoying the scenery. But this sportsman was coming over to me frequently, asking me to dance. Each time I politely said "no".

Eventually, I told him that it was 9pm and I was going to catch the bus home. He grabbed my waist quite strongly and slurred that I was going to miss an amazing night. I removed his hands, said goodbye and went to get on the bus.

A male friend kindly offered to go with me to make sure I got home safe. I thanked him, but I told him I was fine. I was at an official event, surrounded by lots of people, including fellow athletes, who I knew well. I felt completely safe. Normally, I would go home with other female athletes to make sure we were together, but I had no reason to feel unsafe in this environment.

I got on the bus, joining two other international athletes I didn't know and was busy texting Shara on WhatsApp as we travelled home. I was exhausted but happy.

Through the dark days of London, with little money and dealing with my recovery from severe injury in Loughborough, I had emerged on the other side, as a medal-winning athlete. I had a world-class coach who I knew could get me to perform on the very biggest stages and I was finally living my dream. I sat back and allowed myself a rare moment of pure contentment.

The hotel was old, but nothing that I hadn't experienced many times before on the international circuit. You could hear athletes returning from the night out as the floorboards strained under their footsteps. I was settling down to go to bed, watching a brilliantly brain-numbing selection of reality TV, which was taking my mind off the day job. I was relaxing in my pyjamas, winding down after the day and the hilarious nonsense of *The Real Housewives of Atlanta* and *Beverly Hills* was just what I needed. Suddenly, I looked at my watch. It was 3am and I was still watching trashy TV on my laptop.

I heard someone trying to open my door without knocking but I wasn't seriously worried. I thought it might be one of the girls next door trying to get into the wrong room. The door knob initially rattled softly, then suddenly it was being shaken aggressively.

In a few seconds, the door was forced open. I was lying in bed with the covers up but immediately I sensed who it was. It was the sportsman from the lift. I wasn't scared; I was seriously annoyed. I had a flight to catch tomorrow, he was obviously completely pissed from the free bar at the banquet and I wasn't in the mood for his nonsense.

He was slurring his words, the stink of the alcohol stinging my nostrils. He was sitting on my bed and I told him to sit on a chair, which he eventually did, reluctantly, after protest.

My first thought was: 'I'll try to sober him up and get him out of my room as quickly as I can.' I gave him a bottle of water and told him to drink it. He ignored the water and told me that he had seen the way I was looking at him all night. I was baffled. I hadn't been looking anywhere near him, and, in fact, had repeatedly told him that I didn't want to dance with him.

He told me he wouldn't leave this room until I admitted I liked him. I couldn't help laughing, I was so confused. I refused to say it as it couldn't be further from the truth. I reminded him I had a boyfriend, and I told him I genuinely didn't understand what he was on about. He told me I was lying and that he knew that I liked him. He was obviously annoyed by this so-called rejection.

In a split second, he grabbed me aggressively and suddenly I was scared. It didn't make any sense at all. Now he was holding my wrists tightly and his fingernails were piercing the thin skin on my wrists.

I tried to fight him off as he tried to get on top of me. I had always been renowned for my physical strength on the track, but it was useless against this man. I remember a coach once telling me as a young woman, "Anyika, you're so strong no guy will ever try to rape you." How wrong that man was.

The sportsman told me he didn't know why I was trying to fight it, to just let it happen. I couldn't understand how he could be so strong when he looked so skinny. He pinned me on the bed and, for the first time that night, I felt utterly powerless.

Time really started to move slowly. Later in my career, when I got malaria, was near death and was holding the nurse's hand weakly, I felt that same sensation. I had fought physically as hard as I could, but I had no strength left.

He had my arms pinned with his knees and my wrists were above my head. He had one hand directly on my throat. My body was filled with shock. I tried to scream, but his tight grip made it impossible. He told me to shut up and stop fighting this. I tried to wrestle him off once more, terrified at what was going to happen next. I was in a twisted nightmare that I couldn't stop. Nothing added up. I was completely helpless.

With my last bit of energy, I tried to throw him off me once more. It was hopeless, I was pinned and he wrenched my underwear off.

I went completely numb.

There was suddenly a combination of fear and fatigue and I was ready to accept it.

I thought "Why can't my Dad or God be here to protect me. Why is this happening?" None of it made sense. I hadn't done anything wrong. I was crying uncontrollably. I felt his erect penis brush against my body. My body was convulsing.

Just as the rape was going to take place, I knew that I had one last chance to stop the horror. I had numerous friends who had been sexually assaulted and I didn't want to be another statistic. I was having an out-of-body experience. I was utterly exhausted from physically fighting a sportsman far stronger than me. I no longer had the strength in my arms to hold him off me anymore. I had almost nothing left physically, but I had no choice but to keep going.

I told myself, 'Just keep fighting with everything, Anyika. Fight him. Fight. Fight. Fight.'

For a brief moment, when he was trying to penetrate me, he momentarily released his left knee which was pinning down my right leg. I counted to three, and as he was about to complete the act, I managed to kick him as hard as I could.

The hard bone of my knee connected solidly with his genitals. He screamed in pain and rolled off my body. I jumped off the bed immediately and yelled at him to get out of the room. I stood shaking at what had just happened. I have an image of him almost looking confused as if he was slowly coming to his senses and he realised what he had done.

Stumbling, he went to leave the room, but the door wouldn't open. When he had forced it open, he managed to break the old lock springs in the door. We were locked in. I started banging on the door and screaming, not wanting to be stuck in a room with this man for a second longer. Nobody answered. I was terrified and banged the door until my hands were in agony. He sat on a chair with his head down, not trying to help.

It was 4am and thankfully the hotel concierge was having a late-night smoke break and heard the commotion from the room. He couldn't understand English, but eventually, he managed to contact an emergency locksmith. I was stuck in this room with a man who had attempted to rape me, for one hour while we waited to be released. I still don't understand my train of thought, maybe it's the shock; I find myself trying to help this person.

I get water to sober him up, unsure why I am doing it. He sat there, silent and slumped in a chair.

We sit at opposite ends of the room in silence and a fog of thick anger descends on me. I want to shout at him or kill him. I start to look around the room for weapons, anything at all will do. I can't find a single sharp item, apart from my running spikes which I hold in each hand, ready to slash at his skin if he attacks me again.

He sits with his head bowed, not saying a word. My brain cannot process what has just happened. Why did he want to rape me? What did I do wrong? I know I did nothing wrong, but that doesn't stop my brain trying to rationalise something evil that has just happened to me.

Eventually, a sleepy locksmith prises open the door and the sportsman leaves quickly. The locksmith looks at me bemused and says to be careful with the door, before shuffling off into the night. I close the door and do not feel safe. I don't want to lie on the bed where I was nearly raped, or even be in this bedroom, which is completely tainted by his actions.

I go into the bathroom and I cry myself to exhaustion. I didn't sleep a minute that night, lying on the floor. I placed the chair up against the door and shivered with every creak on the hallway. I was convinced that he was coming back to finish the job.

I took a shower to try and calm myself down. The water is scalding hot and I rub soap on my body furiously as if I can cleanse it from rape. I know that no amount of soap will wipe clean the memory of what has happened. I have been surrounded by male friends my whole life and have enjoyed their banter and friendship. When I least suspected it, I have been attacked.

I just wanted to go home as soon as possible. I eventually get to the airport but I am barely able to think clearly.

Suddenly, I see him, the sportsman, in the departures terminal. I freeze. Then I burst into tears and sprint for the nearest toilet. My eyes are bloodshot as I completely break down in a cubicle. I hear women shouting for me to get out as the queue builds, but I don't care. I stand at the bathroom sink, the cold porcelain acting as an anchor as I stand unsteadily. An elderly lady kindly asks, "Are you ok?" That rhetorical question we all ask people so many times, but are often so ill-equipped to deal with, if the answer comes back negative. I thank her and tell her I am fine. I hear my name on the loudspeaker and I sprint to the gate to catch the flight home.

I didn't know what to do. Who could I tell and how could I explain what happened? I felt that people wouldn't believe me. An athlete defined by her physical strength, pinned helpless to the bed by a drunk sportsman?

I had the option of telling someone, but did I want to be painted as a liar, be subjected to a trial on social media and maybe in court? History had taught me that women, and even fewer black women, were rarely believed after sexual assault.

After years of sacrifice and pain, I had finally achieved a level of success and I didn't want this sickening episode to define my career. Who was going to believe me? Why would a sportsman who knew me try to rape me in a busy hotel? I didn't want to put myself through a prosecution that wouldn't be interested in my story. I had too much to lose, and so little to gain.

I never told a single person in authority, not the police, not British Athletics, not anyone.

I got into my house in Loughborough and opened my kit bag. Usually, at the end of every season, I would try to give away most of my kit to kids that needed it in Liverpool. I couldn't do it with this kit, it was damaged and tainted. Looking at it made me feel sick. I threw it outside and would stare at the bag for ages. I didn't want to have that negativity in the house. Eventually, I emptied my kitbag into a binbag with all of my kit from that trip.

I siphoned some petrol from my car's tank and covered the clothes in it. I was about to light a match and throw it on the clothes, but I started to worry about the neighbours, so I stamped the match out. I had to wait a few days for the bin-men to come, it was a Tuesday and the they came on a Thursday. The kit stayed in a pile, almost tormenting me with the nightmare that had occurred. On Thursday, I threw the bag in the bin and stood and watched the bin lorry crush it to make sure that it was gone forever. The bin-man gave me my wheelie bin back and cheerily said, 'have a nice day', probably wondering why this lady was almost in tears, watching the back of his lorry.

I should have told Rohan. I should have told my family. I should have told Rana, Danielle, Caroline or Shara. I should have told anyone. But I didn't. I kept this horrible secret to myself. I moved onto the next season and competed as normal. You might have seen me on television, competing and smiling at the meetings around the world, with little idea that I was crying throughout the night, holding this terrible secret.

I couldn't fall asleep properly. I had constant nightmares of him pinning me down and his hot breath on me. I'd wake up in a pool of sweat. I never felt safe in hotels at international events, insisting that I shared with people that I knew.

I would see the sportsman again, from time to time. As soon as I saw him, I would go to the toilet and cry. I'd splash my face with water. Nobody ever noticed anything.

Shortly after the assault happened, I travelled to compete in Morocco for the Continental Cup and attended the after-party with my teammates Tiffany Porter and James Ellington. Although the season was finished, I wasn't in the mood to drink and was sticking to soft drinks. An athlete I didn't know asked me to dance, putting his hand on my waist. I said no and immediately got a sickening flashback. He then wrapped his arms around me and asked suggestively was I going to come back to his room. I shoved him off and instantly felt paranoid. I felt like my safety was being compromised, so I stayed close to my friends throughout the night.

I told myself to act normal every time I saw him and largely, I did. If you had seen us together, you would never have suspected anything was wrong. I wasn't stopping for a long chat, but I was able to conduct myself professionally. I thought of murdering him, or at least exposing him, but I never did. I hit the weight room hard, trying to get bigger and stronger, lifting heavier weights every session. I felt the need to defend myself should it ever happen again.

As the years went on, I saw him fairly regularly, and, when I did, I made sure that our meeting was brief. At one of the last athletics meetings of my professional career, I had to once again deal with him, albeit in not quite as direct a way.

I was toasting the end of the event and then, with the night coming to a close I went back to my room and saw two friends who said that the same sportsman was in a drunken state and he was trying it on with another female athlete. I felt my anxiety hit the roof.

I asked the girls what room he was staying in, pretending that he had borrowed my phone charger. Once I found it, I sat by his room for hours. I wanted to be there to protect the female in question. I didn't know her, but it didn't matter. I wanted to be there for her, as there was nobody there for me.

I eventually fell asleep in the corridor of the hotel, and

at 5am was woken up by somebody, not unreasonably, asking me what I was doing. I quickly said I was speaking to my boyfriend late in the corridor and had fallen asleep. I wasn't ready to leave the corridor, just in case he returned. I desperately wanted to give the female athlete the protection I had never had. I was terrified for her, just thinking that she might be pinned down helpless in his room.

I know now I needed to say something about this monster, but I never did.

I truly wish I had.

15

Hurt

THERE'S A curious relationship between an athlete and a coach. Of course, we appreciate their technical know-how and ability to squeeze out the extra tenth of a second we might need on the track, but ultimately, it's a business relationship. They provide a service, and they are handsomely paid for it. It's a transaction for some athletes, nothing more and nothing less. I was completely different.

I needed more from my coach than a stopwatch and a barking voice; I needed a mental push as much as a physical one. At times, staying in a dingy hotel room and competing on an unknown track for most of the year, I needed emotional support. In Rana I got what I paid for, technical excellence and the ability to finally realistically visualise standing on an Olympic podium, but rarely anything beyond that.

By 2015, Rana had left his job with UK Athletics, and was now based in Holland, working as a coach for the Dutch Athletics Federation. Typically, he'd left Britain in a blaze of smoke with a parting shot at some UK athletes he felt were cruising through the motions. "Maybe they get comfortable. Maybe they get the funding. Maybe they're big fish in a small pond and that's the way they like it."

Unable to drop my life and move everything to Holland, due to the huge cost, emotionally and financially, I kept working with Rana in a long-distance coaching relationship that just about functioned. I missed the close working relationship that we had built up in Loughborough with the extended Tumbleweed group, where he knew exactly what to say to spark my performance to the next level.

I was now regularly sending out lots of texts and emails asking for the following week's work out from Rana. If I hadn't heard anything, I would normally send out a frantic text on Sunday night. I always tried to keep it breezy and casual, to disguise my anxiety and anger that yet again I didn't have any direction from the man I was paying to coach me.

I'd text, "Hey coach, hope you're good, looking forward to Monday's session. Let me know when it's sent through."

More often than not on a Monday morning there would be nothing in my inbox from him.

I felt like a PhD student asking for guidance on their detailed thesis from a temperamental, but extremely gifted, professor. I was desperate to learn from him but was not getting the materials I needed.

Sometimes, a quick workout would come on Monday in Rana's trademark curt prose. I would follow his workouts

Above: The London 2012 Olympic trials were one of the hardest I had to compete in. I was mentally and physically fried at this point as I was still grieving the loss of my Dad but this moment when I made the team made it all worth it

Left: Taking part in a pre-London 2012 photoshoot with some of my fellow Team GB athletes

Right: Myself, Allyson Felix of the USA, centre, and Italy's Gloria Hooper, right, in action in the women's 200m heats at London 2012

Above and right: I was determined to enjoy the closing ceremony of London 2012. It was a difficult year for me but I made some incredible memories at the Games, such as seeing my sporting idol, Serena Williams, casually chilling in the Olympic Village!

Left: Can you tell I was elated to become British 200m champion? 2013 was a great season for me as I was one of only three women in the world to have the world championship qualifying standard for the 100m, 200m and 400m

Left: Friday night lights. Competing in the 4x100m at a packed stadium at the London Anniversary Games, July 2013. I loved competing in the sprint relay and more so on this day as we went on to win the race

Left: Me and Shara back in our room after receiving our medals at the World Championships in Beijing, August 2015. I couldn't have been more proud of us. She was my roommate and one of my biggest supporters for years so to see both of us winning a medal was pretty special

Above: Myself, Christine Ohuruogu, Eilidh Child and Seren Bundy-Davies celebrate after finishing third in Beijing. However, my smiles were hiding a lot of physical and mental trauma...

Above: I had a habit of closing my eyes during the last few metres in a 400m. The pain of lactic acid was unreal but even more satisfying when you win

Below: Seren Bundy-Davies, Eilidh Doyle, myself and Emily Diamond celebrate after winning the 4x400m relay at the 2016 European Athletic Championships at the Olympic Stadium, Amsterdam. After this win, I had a feeling we were about to do something special a month later

Both: Indeed we were! My face says it all as I join Christine Ohuruogu, Emily and Eilidh on the podium with our bronze medals in the 4x400m relay at Rio 2016. This moment was a culmination of a dream for me, and a moment that made all the pain and sacrifices worth it

Above: Celebrating the success of Team GB after the Rio Olympics at the Team GB homecoming in Manchester in October 2016 with fellow medallists, left to right; Asha Philip, Emily Diamond, and Jessica Ennis-Hill

Below: Myself and Jurgen Klopp. I was invited by Liverpool to attend one of their first games of the season. He told me he had watched my race in Rio and was extremely proud of me for bringing back a medal to Liverpool

Above: Just trying to take it all in – and make memories for life – at the parade in Manchester

Left: Receiving my honorary fellowship from John Moores University in 2017. As a former graduate of JMU, it was a huge honour to be recognised for my achievement from the people who helped me along the way

Right: Like I said, I had a habit of closing my eyes the closer I got to the finish line and this time in the pouring rain! Competing in the 400m as Team Captain in the 2018 Commonwealth Games

Above: Parading the Commonwealth Torch around Anfield at half-time during a game in 2017. I loved every second of it – and we beat Crystal Palace 1-0!

Left: Competing in the European Championships in Berlin in 2018. Berlin is an iconic stadium and the fans in Germany always showed love to track and field

Below: Eilidh Doyle, Zoey Clark, Amy Allcock and myself celebrate our bronze success in Berlin

Below: Hoping to inspire the next generation as I deliver a motivational speech to schoolchildren in Liverpool. I always find the greatest joy in sharing my story with others, especially young people

Above: Meeting Mauricio Pochettino and Harry Kane at a warm weather training camp in Barcelona in 2018. The Spurs team were also there for warm weather training. Myself and Harry exchanged training tips even though I'm a Liverpool fan!

exactly to a tee and worked under one of his former assistants, Graham Hedman, in Loughborough, but nothing could replace having Rana trackside. If the workouts didn't come, Graham and I just improvised. Like a boxer needing their cornerman between each round, reassuring them that they are winning the round; I needed Rana to push me to my absolute limits.

Athletics is a brutally lonely sport at times, and it's no coincidence that I eventually thrived in British relay teams or amongst the easy training banter of Tumbleweed. By 2015, Tumbleweed had blown in different directions, with some British athletes choosing to stay in Loughborough for continuity, while others moved to Holland with Rana.

When finances allowed, I would drive all the way to the Dutch Olympic Training Centre in the small town of Papendal and, on tired legs that had been pumping the clutch and brake pedals, I would try to get through gruelling sessions.

I never experienced what most people would consider financial security in my career, but 2015 finally provided some rewards and it ended up being one of my most lucrative seasons. I was running well enough to get invited to regular Diamond League races and give myself some financial stability and recognition at the top end of the sport.

I was confident moving into the World Championships in Beijing, believing that I could absolutely win a medal in the 4x400 relay and reach the final of the individual 400 metres.

With its own unique timing, in a familiar theme of my career, my body started to break down when I needed it most. Just before I arrived in Japan for the pre-Championship holding camp, I was nursing an achilles injury that needed frequent therapy, to the point where UK Athletics wanted to send me home from the holding camp before we even got to the World Championships.

It is always a gamble to take an injured athlete to one of the major championships if they are not fully fit, as the resourcing of therapists may not be worth the outlay on a potential lame duck. Our team doctor Dr Rob rang Rana while I was sitting within earshot, "I'll have to be honest, while it's not the worst achilles I've seen, it doesn't look great at all and we're going to have to think of sending Anyika home."

I interrupted Rob immediately. "Dr Rob, I just want to let you know that I'm not going anywhere, we're not booking no plane ticket, and you're definitely not sending me back to the UK. We are going to fix this, and that's the end of it."

He told me that we had to consider our options, and I agreed, as long as the options involved me working on getting fit enough to compete. I went and had lunch while the medical staff conferred on my situation. I had seen similar situations play out so many times; if an athlete is not right physically, the easiest option is to send them home. I refused to make it easy for them to take me to the airport.

I returned to the medical room and was met by my physio

James Davies and Dr Rob. Dr Rob looked slightly more relaxed and gave me the news. "We had a conversation with Rana, and after a bit of thought on how we can tackle this injury, you don't need to go home. I'll warn you, to get you even near ready, it's going to be very intense, and could be very painful. You will have to stick to this plan religiously for the next seven days until we get to Beijing. Are you ready for all of this?"

I nodded happily. It was a small victory, but a meaningful one.

Together we created a plan to coax the inflammation on my burning achilles tendon down to a manageable level that would eventually allow me to compete. I couldn't run properly on a track for five days, so my workouts were completed in the hotel pool and on the exercise bike.

I was preparing for the World Championships, flanked by elderly holidaymakers, enjoying a leisurely lap of the pool after their cocktail hour while I was desperately fighting to keep my season intact.

Despite being an elite athlete for over a decade, ironically, I have never had a great pain threshold away from the track. When my body was burning with crippling lactic acid in the last 50 metres of the 400 metres, I hated it, but I could deal with it as it was my job.

Away from athletics, I will do anything to avoid unnecessary pain. As part of the medical schedule to keep me taped together ahead of Beijing, I endured a shock wave gun that spits like an angry cricket on a hot summer night and basically charges electric current into your injured leg. With every spit of the gun, I would feel like a boiling hot steak knife was being plunged into my tendon and scream in agony. I tried to imagine that the gun was slowly stitching the damaged threads of my tendon back together. I was in the medical room six times a day, dreading every visit, but knowing this was what needed to be done.

I could just about walk without hobbling when I finally arrived in Beijing, and the normal excitement of competing in a World Championships was replaced with fears that I would be unable to get beyond a 50-metre hobble. The fact that I was even competing was a surprise and there was nothing expected from me from the team. I also developed intense period pain that added to the strain and anxiety of competition.

When it came to competing, I got the physio to apply the strapping as tight as possible, painting it with makeup to stop it standing out and making it too noticeable to my competitors.

My sport is a strange one. There are championships that you can train perfectly for and be in peak physical condition, but, in just over 50 seconds, the smallest thing goes wrong, you run a terrible race and your year is defined by it. Your hamstring could go, or you could have a severe panic attack at the starting line.

Anything can and does happen. Conversely, you can go

into the World Championships, strapped up and hobbling like a Granny on day release from the nursing home, doubled up in pain and run some of the best events of your life, which is exactly what happened to me.

I walked out for the first heat of the individual 400 metres gingerly, swirling slightly from the cocktail of a humid Beijing morning and the effects of a strong dose of Ibuprofen. I didn't know how far my achilles could be pushed, after a week of working out in the company of pensioners, enjoying their golden years abroad. I told myself that I had nothing to lose, I said my usual prayer, Psalm 23. Suddenly I felt a sense of calmness and peace.

Regardless of the injury, I knew I was in the form of my life and I was completely free to express myself on the track. I started to enjoy myself, almost masochistically. This injury had just become another challenge that I was going to conquer. I qualified for the semi-final, feeling no pain in the achilles throughout the lap of the track, although it started to burn as soon as the adrenaline had worn off.

Just as we walked to the call room, Rana gave me a pep talk. The game had changed, and there were high expectations which I knew I had to achieve. It wasn't just a race, it was about defining myself in the most difficult of times.

He told me I was ready to run a 50-second time. I never looked at my competitors before we lined up, but he said that I was in good company in a hot semi-final, and now was the time to join them at their level. If Rana had one amazing ability, it was to bring out the best in his athletes exactly when it mattered most, delivering their best performances in major championships.

Looking down at my makeup splattered strapping, doubled in pain, with an achilles that felt like it was going to explode, I was ready to prove the world wrong. I looked around the call room and I saw Allyson Felix of the United States and Shericka Jackson of Jamaica. I finally felt like I belonged in their company. We were about to compete in the final of three semi-finals, and I glanced at the television to see Christine win her semi-final with a season best time of 50.16. I was elated for her, she had form just when it mattered. As usual, without realising it, Christine gave me a level of calmness and composure before I stepped on the track, only this time I was alone.

When I walked out to the track, I felt the sharp shooting pain of my achilles. I ignored it, and told myself to focus on running the perfect race. I never felt pain when I ran in Beijing. As ever, regardless of the stage, the track provided me with a sanctuary from pain, whether mental or physical. I considered this World Championship a metaphor for how I wanted to live my life. I had put my body through hell and refused to give up without a fight.

Rana had briefed me that Allyson would make a quick start, and as usual she did. Her smooth and graceful running style cut through her competitors with ease, and I could see her trademark high white socks in the distance after 200 metres. I was in the inside lane, telling my mind to keep calm, and to try to keep Allyson within range as I entered the last 120 metres.

When you turn that last bend into the final sprint, your brain will search for anything to give you inspiration to keep fighting to the finish line. I heard Rana in my mind, "Just put yourself into contention, Anyika." I was still fighting for third, duelling with the Jamaican Novlene Williams-Mills, with Allyson and Shericka ahead of us. My mind and heart were clear and had more to give, but my legs were failing me. I slipped into fourth place, holding, and I sensed that my legs were going to give way. I had nothing left and was beaten to fifth place by the Ukrainian Nataliya Pyhyda who was banned from the sport for two years in 2009 for testing positive for the steroid stanozolol.

I ran a career best time of 50.87, delighted with my time and devastated that it hadn't been enough to reach the final. I congratulated all of the girls in the race, apart from Pyhyda, who I refused to acknowledge.

I have dealt with drug cheats my whole career, and it never gets easier to understand. You fight to do the right thing, in competition and training, fighting to push your body an extra inch if it gives you an edge. When you have been involved in this sport, you know that sadly there is an inevitability that you are competing against bona fide cheats. Whether they are associated with certain agents, coaches, training camps, or even sophisticated doping regimes like

Russia, you know what you are up against at the highest level.

In my whole career, I can honestly say I was never offered drugs once, but that didn't mean that I wasn't under serious scrutiny. My body was constantly examined on internet forums, and newsprint. If my body was more muscular, or too lean, I was accused of taking drugs. My answer was simple. If I was taking drugs, I must have had the world's worst chemist. I should have sacked them a lot earlier for failing to get me more individual medals.

You cannot get publicly angry or confrontational about the injustice of a competitor that has cheated, or is cheating, competing in your race. The hatred will eat you up, and leave you helpless. You just hope and pray that by running clean, and training as hard as you possibly can, you are still able to beat them. I always knew that I could look myself, and my parents, in the mirror and know that I had done everything correctly.

Generally, with someone like Pyhyda, they are not acting alone, they are part of a far larger and sophisticated system. I remember the evolution of the Russian female athletes at the start of my career in the 2006 European Championships in Gothenburg, who were doing superhuman feats on the track and field. We all had suspicions, they were dominating too many events, but nobody could prove anything. If we complained we would have been accused of being poor losers.

It became more blatant, and more arrogant. There were

reports of Russian syringes and drugs being found in stadium bins. There was clear evidence, but still nobody got caught. You'd sit in countless call rooms knowing that you were sitting knee to knee with dopers. These women who were doping were part of a system – if they didn't want to take part, there were countless others who were ready to step into the breach. If you are young, impressionable and poor, and are offered a good income and adulation to be the world's best, what do you do?

You saw these Russian female athletes come and go, as disposable in that system as the discarded syringes in the bin. There were always new cogs ready to be placed into the machine. I was angry at the sanction systems that enabled this doping, and also furious at the international governing bodies for letting it happen for so many years on their watch. I also felt frustration at the way an athlete returned from suspension from doping without an inch of contrition. Like so many athletes, I was in a fight with one arm tied behind my back. The odds were stacked against us, but we wanted to run clean and did so.

The happy memory of running a personal best in the semi final dissipated with the prickly pain of my achilles. After a few days of torture under the shock wave gun, I had to take a taxi from the hotel to my sponsor Adidas' hospitality tent. We were given cards printed in Mandarin to show to the driver so he would know exactly how to get back to our hotel. After completing a supermarket sweep with a mound of fresh kit, I stood outside on a steamy humid Beijing August night for an hour, to be ignored by every single taxi that went by. I put out my hand and waved, wondering if this generic international sign language was not translating in this huge and bustling city.

Finally, a kind white British man noticed what was happening to me and stood beside me. He explained that he had been living in the city for the last year and unfortunately, this wasn't uncommon. Nobody would stop for me because of my skin colour. He hailed a taxi, a car immediately stopped beside him and he quickly asked if I could hold his hand. I nodded, confused, and he held my hand as we both got into the taxi. He quickly explained in Mandarin where I needed to go and then got out of the car in one swift motion. I wasn't angry at the blatant racism, unfortunately, it was just another day on the international circuit. I had grown wearily used to it. I just wanted to get home and rest ahead of the 4x400 relay final.

In an attempt to spice up the relay events for the crowd, the IAAF decided that each country in the final had to make a special entrance before the race. I think they were trying to bring a bit of the pre-game razzle dazzle of the NBA or the NFL with none of the budget. Still, if it attracted a few more spectators and interest, then I was all for it. There were little kids who would clap us in, then we would briefly stand as a four, and pose. It was cringe, but also just silly enough to be the perfect ice breaker for our nerves. I stood with Christine, Eilidh Doyle and Seren Bundy-Davies as we did a quick Royal wave that paled into insignificance with the strutting confidence of the American team and their slick *Charlie's Angels* pose.

In the call room, while every other country was concentrating on their relay changeover, the USA team were arguing about who was going to go, in what formation, for their carefully choreographed *Charlie's Angel* routine. In Sanya Richards-Ross and Allyson Felix, they had two of the quickest women in the world, not overly concerned about beating the Jamaicans, but arguing over who got to do Cameron Diaz's iconic pistol pose in the middle of the group.

In such an individual sport, the relays are to our sport what the Ryder Cup is to golf, or the Davis Cup is to tennis; a rare opportunity to work with some of your biggest rivals as a team. Even after all these years, I still loved competing with Christine. She had been there and done it all and having her there always brought me a sense of peace. An Olympic and World Champion that I had known as a teenager, who I was now going to take the baton from in the second leg, assured me that all was going to be well.

The pain from my achilles had sharpened, and the makeup painted strapping was still a key part of my kit, but its pain was bearable. Horrible, but bearable. We knew that the Americans and Jamaicans were incredible competitors, but we had full faith that we could hold our own and we did.

As predicted, the Americans and Jamaicans ran far out

in front, but the British team managed to come together perfectly to come third. I look at the footage now of me taking the baton from Christine, and I am amazed at how relaxed I look, given what was at stake and the agony of my achilles. For just over 50 seconds, I was able to savour the rare joy that comes from a job well done in athletics at the highest level.

I hugged Christine and my teammates at the finish line, oblivious to the Jamaicans celebrating after beating the Americans in a closely contested race. It would be my first and only World Championship medal and it is something that I still cherish, as it reminds me that anything is possible when you find the strength to push through mental and physical pain.

I wanted to cry, I was so drained emotionally and physically. I held onto Christine, and my body shook. I realised I had discovered strength that I didn't know I had physically and mentally. All of the doubts, barely being able to walk to the starting line, and then running on adrenaline to bring it together at the World Championships.

The human body is a truly amazing thing, even when it is battered and bruised, through sheer will, it can go places that you never imagined it could.

You learn to savour these rare and beautiful moments of joy when you are an athlete. I could barely walk to the athletes' banquet in Beijing to celebrate the close of the championships, but it didn't matter. Our team stayed up talking and drinking all night long, reliving the race, and just hoping that this night didn't end too quickly. We went right through the night and didn't sleep, leaving the hotel with our bags at 6.30am to catch our flight home.

After winning bronze in the World Championships, my life on the track was finally going to plan, but off it, I felt completely lost at times. I was training at the HiPAC in Loughborough, in familiar settings that had become increasingly uncomfortable.

I noticed that they had decided to brand the centre with posters of celebrated British athletes that could inspire the next generation to hopefully follow in their footsteps. I also noticed that there wasn't a single black British female athlete on the walls.

Every day I walked into training, I thought about a young black woman starting her career and dreaming of competing for her country. What message was this sending out to her? You cannot see it, so how on earth can you be it?

In the main training centre for British athletes, not only were we lacking black leaders at management level, but we also had no sense of representation in terms of the achievement of countless black female athletes past and present, who had won medals at the highest level of competition for their country.

I felt a range of complex emotions training in Loughborough, ranging from invisibility and ultra-visibility. When I walked into the centre, I looked around, it was a rare sight to see a black female athlete training there and I felt completely visible, but for the wrong reasons.

It hadn't always been the case, particularly in the days of Tumbleweed, when Rana's rambling gang of athletes from across the world had added to the noise and flair of this English university town. The invisibility came from the lack of representation and appreciation of black female athletes, who sacrificed everything to represent their country. Paula Dunn was the first female senior coach in UK Athletics, and, in her role as chief of the Paralympic programme, she was the only black representative at senior management level.

Before Paula, there had never been a black person in senior management in UK Athletics. A talented former sprinter, Paula was also an exceptional person, with far too much weight on her shoulders, from dealing with black athletes who had nobody else to confide in. Paula was responsible for driving a huge Paralympic programme, buoyed by the success of London 2012, while also taking on the unpaid and unrecognised responsibility of representing a huge section of athletes that weren't directly under her care.

Left with no choice, I pulled Paula aside and pointed to the posters on display in the centre. "Paula, where are we?" I asked. "Where are the black women?" Paula listened patiently and promised that it would be flagged accordingly. As usual, she would get it sorted out.

Eventually, I was summoned into a meeting where the mood was formal and sombre. I felt as if I was back at high school, and I was called to see the head teacher for graffitiing my name under the table, with Paula as the supportive teacher vouching for me. I sat down and waited for what they had to say while also being more than willing to convey my thoughts.

I explained that it wasn't just about posters, it was about recognition of the large numbers of black female athletes who needed to feel welcome, and, most importantly, acknowledged, within the system. I wasn't asking for much, I was just asking for a simple change in posters in the centre to recognise the huge contribution that we had made to UK Athletics currently, and historically.

The centre's success had been based, to some degree, on the efforts and hard work of black female athletes and all I wanted was for those athletes to feel represented around the place; to be made to feel like we were as important and as integral as we clearly were.

I was not asking for that much, I stated my case clearly and fairly and it seemed to be a fairly obvious and important issue that needed bringing up. To my mind, the meeting was not a success. It left me with a feeling that my efforts and messages would be ignored.

I am rarely lost for words, but this time I was completely silenced. I felt a hot anger seep through my body. I felt completely misunderstood. I just couldn't – and still don't – see the problem.

My opinion – then and now – is that black female athletes

were a mainstay of athletics so, surely, black female athletes should feel visible? That was the only point I wanted to make but it was crystal clear that it was a point that was failing to hit home

I didn't know whether to cry, or yell. Paula immediately looked over at me, and begged me with her eyes to keep calm, which – somehow – I did. I didn't say anything and avoided eye contact. I just walked out of the office. Thanks to Paula, the posters were eventually sorted out, with a selection of Britain's female black athletes hoisted high on the walls. Although it did take them over a year to do it.

Once again, Paula was having to do work far beyond her remit. I still don't understand why I needed to point out what seemed a simplistic issue of acknowledgement.

It was never about posters. It was about a bigger picture of not feeling valued by the organisation that you and your friends have sacrificed everything for and, in many cases, have endured untold horrors to wear their country's colours.

I never felt protected by the system before and certainly not after this incident. How was I expected to tell these so-called leaders about my experiences of racism and two brutal sexual assaults? The truth is, I never could have. So I didn't.

As a result of how isolated I began to feel, my relationship with UK Athletics became strictly about business, there was no warmth or higher sense of purpose from competing for your country.

Although I still passionately loved my sport as much as ever, I was a cog in their machine that needed to churn out medals to keep the high executive salaries paid on time. UK Athletics provided the platform for me to compete and the best possible training facilities. I would turn up at the HiPAC, train to the very best of my ability, and leave.

I wouldn't even interact with people if I could avoid it, my headphones were constantly on. I always felt a strong responsibility to be completely professional at all times, no matter how hard it felt.

Just under a year until the Olympics, and I was almost completely disenfranchised from the UK Athletics machine. The pride I felt in competing for my country never died, but loyalty to the organisation that administered the sport was completely lost forever.

We are taught about the sacrifice of competing for your country in the Olympics and the beauty of it, but if you don't feel protected or valued while doing it, what is the point? I was now simply there to get a job done and that's what I intended to do.

16

Malaria

THE CONGOLESE nurse holds my hand and softly tells me that I'm not going to die on her watch.

I lie on a bed of ice, completely helpless, surrounded by a soaking wet floor and choose to believe her. I have built a career based on my physical strength and conditioning, now I am dependent on the skill of the medical professionals at St John & St Elizabeth hospital in north London to keep me alive.

How did it even come to this? At the end of the season, after fighting through the World Championships to win bronze, my body and mind desperately needed a rest. I decided to visit my family in Nigeria for a short holiday, before joining Rohan for a long-awaited romantic break to the Dominican Republic. After a long season of regimented workouts and disciplined diets, I gorged on food and basked in the sun, completely carefree. It was fun to let loose before the hard work started again.

After a few days in the hotel in the Dominican Republic, I started to feel dizzy, but put it down to nothing more than overindulging. I wasn't going crazy, but my body tended to be extremely sensitive to any change in diet or routine. It's a bit like changing a finely tuned car's petrol from premium unleaded to the cheap stuff. It might start stuttering a little bit, but it will still function, just about. I got through the final few days of the holiday but also noticed that my urine was now dark and got a little more concerned.

During a cabaret show, I couldn't get comfortable, feeling a cool blast of air wherever I sat, as if I was sitting directly under an icy air vent. I asked Rohan where the cold air was coming from, convinced that there must be stealthy air conditioning units somewhere and he looked at me confused. The temperature was over 30 degrees on a sticky Caribbean night, and I was shivering manically, huddled against him to get some warmth into my body.

Any athlete will tell you that we learn to live in a world of pain. I had almost forgotten what it feels like to compete or train without a niggle, so I just put the dizziness and change of urine down to a bug.

Maybe the hotel buffet hadn't agreed with me. I did email Dr Rob from UK Athletics and explained the symptoms, more to get it on the radar. I trained as soon as I got back to Loughborough and felt sluggish around the track. Again, I wondered if it was too much holiday indulgence, or perhaps something more serious. Dr Noel Pollock from the HiPAC insisted on taking a blood and urine sample, so after that was done, I hopped in the car and went home.

I started shaking as soon as I got in the car, my teeth were chattering manically and I was sweating buckets through my training gear. I got home and slowly stumbled up the stairs and dived into bed, pulling two thick blankets over me. I was freezing cold, but I could also feel the temperature of my body rise. It was a fever like I had never experienced. I turned on my bedside radio to listen to Chelsea playing Dynamo Kyiv in a Champion's League game.

I was drifting in and out of consciousness, but trying to focus on the game, simply to have a distraction. Despite not supporting Chelsea, I was listening for the most minute details from the commentary, trying to find something in the game that would take me away from this pain. In times of distress, the sounds of football reminded me of happy times with my Dad at home in Liverpool. Now I was alone in Loughborough freezing, sweating and unsure what was wrong.

I barely slept and hallucinated throughout the night. I was bitterly cold, but my bedsheets were completely drenched in sweat. I put my hand on my sweaty forehead and knew that this was more than a run of the mill fever. The next morning Dr Noel rang me and told me that my blood and urine was showing kidney failure and I needed to get to St John & St Elizabeth Hospital as soon as possible.

I barely had the strength to get out of bed and had nobody

to take me to London. All of my friends were out training and Rohan was already working in London. The only course of action was to get into my car and drive. Should UK Athletics have sent someone to help me get there, given the severity of my condition? Almost certainly. I asked if they could pay for a taxi, but they said that unfortunately, it wasn't possible.

I went into a fight or flight response, almost like running in the World Championships a few months before with my makeup splattered strapping. Except this time, I wasn't trying to beat the clock to win a medal, I was racing to save my life.

Before I got into the car, I started praying. I just prayed that I would get to the hospital safe and well. Then I started to utilise my training as an athlete to set out a game plan of how to get to my destination.

In good traffic, it will take two and a half hours by car from Loughborough to London. I knew that regardless of how ill I was feeling, I had to only think about positive thoughts. I'd go through tiny details of things that I loved from my holiday. Anything to take me away from the increasing pain in my body.

I started driving and couldn't stop, I was convinced that if I did, I would collapse on a hard shoulder, unable to continue the journey. I was still shivering and freezing cold, and my car heater was working at full capacity but still not taking the edge off the fever. My whole body was shaking and I was gripping the steering wheel tightly to stay upright. The pain was brutal, but just about manageable.

It was another challenge for me to overcome. I would turn

the car radio up to full volume and wind the window down, just to keep me focused on anything but counting down the miles until London.

Somehow, I drove continuously until I was forced to stop at a service station in Watford, desperate for the toilet, giving me my last opportunity to stop before I got off the M1. When I got back in the car, the previous symptoms I experienced became turbo charged. I had a high fever, a cramped stomach and a pounding migraine that clamped its claws into every fibre of my brain. The drive from Watford to St John's Wood would normally be a leisurely half an hour, but this time, I felt every single second of the journey as I hunched over the steering wheel in excruciating agony.

After the longest three-hour drive of my life, I parked at St John's High Street, opened the door and immediately collapsed onto the street. The smartly dressed shoppers all stopped to see what the commotion was and some asked if I needed help. I should have said that yes, I urgently needed an ambulance, but even feeling near death I exercised my British right not to cause undue fuss, and lied that I was ok.

I can see that that was stupid on my part, but I was disorientated and embarrassed. Amongst the artisan butchers and bakeries, St John's Wood rarely has black women sprawled flat on its pavements near death. I knew that I was causing a scene and wanted to stop it immediately.

I used all my strength to get up, and the normally brisk two-minute walk to the hospital from the car park took me 20 minutes as I stumbled, hanging onto lamp posts and railings on the street like a crazy woman. Eventually, I reached reception and was immediately taken to see a kidney specialist who said that I didn't look good at all, understating the situation just slightly.

Every time he gently prodded my stomach, I felt like a sharp shard of glass was slicing into my internal organs. The pain was becoming increasingly unbearable, but I surprised myself by asking the doctor what meds he needed to get me on, because I needed to get out of here to train for the Rio Olympics. He looked at me, stunned, unable to comprehend just how naïve I was about my health.

Although at this stage I didn't know that I was potentially near death, I did know that something was seriously wrong with my body, but yet my first concern wasn't dying, it was missing two days of training and having to break the news to Rana. This is the essence of a high-performance athlete, you become so blinkered in your approach that normal ideas of perspective get completely lost.

I hate hospitals, but really, who likes them? They can remind you of the happiness of a birth, but so often, they are associated with sickness and death. Just being back in a hospital helpless brought back painful memories of my Dad passing in 2012. A strong man, who ended up at the mercy of a doctor's orders and the tubes attached to his body. Like Dad, I had no choice but to trust in the hospital staff, but I was getting more and more worried.

I sat through five hours of tests, my blood was taken, I was put through an MRI machine and I was even given a pregnancy test. I couldn't eat or drink and was getting weaker by the minute. I tried to sleep, but the bright lights tormented me. Eventually, the doctor came to visit me with a beaming smile, as if he had cracked an extremely difficult cryptic crossword puzzle with no help on the clues. "I've got good news for you," he said. I waited. "We've run a pile of tests and finally worked out what it is, you've got a small dose of malaria."

It didn't feel like a small dose. The doctor showed me a scan of the malaria parasites invading my red blood cells. His tone was matter of fact. "As you can see Anyika, the parasites have obviously multiplied in your body rapidly." I could see the tiny organisms moving frantically across my body. I had to stop myself from throwing up all over the hospital floor.

I was on malaria medication the whole time I was in Nigeria, and initially had my doubts that I could have caught it there, but the doctor was absolutely correct. To be precise, I had plasmodium falciparum malaria, one of the deadliest strains possible and gradually, the mood changed in the hospital.

As the day and then the evening wore on, my temperature and sense of fear rose to new levels. A Congolese nurse was starting her shift, she took my hand and calmly told me how grave the situation was becoming.

"Anyika, you have to listen to me carefully my darling,"

she said. "If we cannot get your body temperature down from 40, to at least 37, then you won't make it until next morning."

I wanted to cry, but I was too tired.

"As soon as your temperature goes down you can go to sleep. We have to cool you down, so we can either put you in an ice bath, or we can pack your bed with ice throughout the night. Which one do you want?"

I weakly replied the ice bags, as I couldn't physically move to get into the bath. The clock ticked and the ice quickly melted under the sizzling heat of my body, stripped down to my underwear. I was in tears, scared, but also exhausted. My room in the hospital was covered in water from the melted ice, as my body fried it to liquid almost immediately.

My Congolese guardian angel nurse and Rohan, who had now arrived at the hospital, took turns holding my hand. I barely had the strength to squeeze back.

My whole adult life, I had found a coping mechanism in the idea of reps that take 30 seconds. If I was doing a high intensity workout, I would break everything down to 30 seconds, telling myself that whatever I was going through, I could always get through another few seconds.

I tried to do this as I lay with my bare skin pressed against the jagged bed of ice, but it didn't work. Every time my body burned through a bag of ice, immediately another one would be brought to replace it. This was an endurance feat that my mind couldn't break. I lay there as limp as a rag doll.

I looked at the nurse for reassurance and it almost worked.

This small lady with beautiful, glowing skin was completely in control of her craft. I generally hate calling African women 'strong', as it's often a lazy label but this woman really was, physically and mentally.

She didn't stop all night, hauling huge bags of ice, and heaving my leaden body over them. In tandem with monitoring my temperature, she was constantly soothing my panicked mind by telling me that we were going to get through this night together.

She was speaking words of affirmation. "Anyika, look at me, look at me please, you'll be fine, you've got this." Anytime she left the room to get ice, I'd get nervous and want her back. I became completely dependent, like a child. Anytime I was drifting off to sleep, she'd rouse me. "Hey, Hey! Anyika, stay with me now, please. Do you want a fan on you? Music?" I'd croak to please put on MTV. I'm a visual person, and tried my very best to focus hard on the images of the music videos, largely without success. I was completely in survival mode. I was trying to focus on MTV, the gust from the fans, even the ice burning my skin. Anything to keep me awake.

Rohan rang my Mum in Liverpool and held the speakerphone to my mouth, and I was barely able to reply. "God is with you. Please don't be scared Anyika. I'm coming straight away to be with you."

I could hear the fear and sadness in her voice and I hated that.

I rarely saw my parents cry, or even get very emotional. She had endured months in hospital caring for my Dad only a few years before, now her daughter lay almost dying and out of reach. We were both upset. Mum was upset that she wasn't there in London to protect her daughter and I wanted her there beside me. She protected me as she only knew how, through prayer, reciting a prayer in Igbo that I had known since childhood. There's nothing like a mother's prayer in your time of need.

"Chineke nnam biko nyere Anyika aka ka osi na onya dakwasiri ya bilie. Biko nye ya ike ka odi nma osiso."

"God, please allow Anyika to overcome this illness. Please give her strength to survive this."

I cried because my Mum felt so helpless, and now the reality of what was happening was finally settling in on me. In a vain attempt to stay awake, I played a highlight reel of some of my favourite races in my mind. I thought about the race in Beijing, taking the baton from Christine in a packed Bird's Nest stadium to help the girls win bronze in the World Championships. Only a few weeks ago, this single race had been the most important thing in my life. Now it was completely meaningless.

In 10 months, I was aiming to compete in the Olympic Games and now they were simply trying to keep me alive through the night.

After hours of lying on the spiky mattress of ice bags, my temperature came down enough to grant me a small amount of sleep. I didn't really think of the nurse as a gifted medical professional anymore, she was now my coach, and I needed her direction to win the most important contest yet. I had won a medal in the World Championships and experienced the devastation of letting myself down on the biggest stage of the London Olympics, but in that moment, none of it mattered. I needed the nurse's calming directions to get me through the night alive and I was going to do everything she told me to the letter.

"You're going to be alright Anyika," she soothed me. "Don't worry darling. I know you feel terrible, but I've seen enough of these cases back home to know that you'll be fine. I never let anyone die on my shift and you're not going to be the first, ok?"

The morning came, and I opened my eyes to the most beautiful sunrise I had ever seen overlooking London. My guardian angel nurse had gone home while I had grabbed a rare and precious amount of sleep. It had been another night's work for her, but she had helped to save my life.

Dr Noel arrived at the hospital at 5pm to help transfer me to the Hospital for Tropical Diseases in London for further observation and treatment. There was nobody else to take me to hospital, so Noel had to wheel me into reception just before starting a family holiday. Just before he left, I almost begged him to stay with me, but I knew that I couldn't.

I had to recover, and very gradually my condition improved. Doctors asked me how I was feeling, and I would tell them that I was feeling better, but I wanted to know when I could leave and return to training for the Olympics. They would look at me like I was mad and they were right. Later, an infectious disease expert told me that he wasn't sure how my strain of malaria had avoided my kidneys; if I had waited 12 more hours to go to the hospital they said I definitely would have died.

My career as an athlete was hanging by a thread. I had to teach myself how to walk again and I devised my own training session in the hospital corridor. I would try and walk 15 metres without stopping. It was difficult at first to move without grabbing the guardrails, but soon, I was able to walk around the whole hospital corridors with my drip attached.

The pristine track of the Olympic Stadium in Rio would have to wait, I was content to shuffle around the hospital lino floor in my carpet slippers, accelerating past elderly patients with tennis balls on their zimmer frames. I could only imagine what my competitors would think if they saw me shuffling around the hospital.

After eventually being discharged after eight days, I visited a consultant to ask him what my chances were of returning to training. He looked at me confused. "Training for what Anyika?" he asked. I told him for the Olympics. He paused briefly and looked me in the eye. "Anyika, there's no easy way of telling you this, but you were incredibly close to being on dialysis for life. You just need to focus on looking after yourself and putting the Olympics to one side. After what your organs have been through, you need to put all of your focus into just living a normal, healthy life."

I burst into tears. I was eternally grateful to the amazing medical staff that had kept me alive but devastated that my career seemed to be over. I turned to Google for solace, frantically looking up athletes with kidney problems, with the late, great, New Zealand rugby player Jonah Lomu and the former Manchester United striker Andy Cole coming up. I was desperate for any hope and to see whether these athletes had been able to compete at the highest level after they'd recovered.

Ultimately, I was confused and didn't know where to turn. I stupidly went onto Instagram, as much for a distraction as anything, but its carefully curated stream of teammates on the track getting ready for Rio just painted an unpleasant contrast to my new reality.

I returned home to Liverpool to live for a month. I was 32 years old and back living in my teenage bedroom, as far away from the HiPAC as possible and that suited me perfectly.

Through my mother's love and guidance, I found the self-belief to not give up on Rio. Most of the staff and athletes on the team had no clue where I was, or know anything about my condition and I simply told them that I needed to be at home with family and was training in Liverpool.

This was true, I was training back home, but rather than sprinting around athletics tracks, I was slowly walking laps of the back garden.

I sometimes slept in the same bed as my Mum. When I was younger and the house in Dingle was under threat of getting attacked, I would find comfort in my parents snoring. It reminded me that even when everything else felt out of control, they were still there protecting me. As an adult, I again found solace in simply being close to my Mum.

At times, I felt on the edge of a breakdown and my Olympic dreams were in pieces. Lying awake, and hearing Mum's snores, I knew that whatever happened to my career, she was always going to be with me.

Gradually, after a month back home in Liverpool I was able to move from walking in the garden to light jogging and returned to Loughborough to complete my recovery. I told teammates that I had been recovering from a few niggles and was working my way up to full fitness.

I had been in regular contact with Rana throughout my recovery, and when I returned to Loughborough his reaction was telling, saying "You better not go back to Nigeria again."

Part of my reticence in talking about my malaria diagnosis to teammates or the wider track and field family was due to my fear that Nigeria, and by extension Africa, would be unfairly tarnished.

I had heard enough unfair criticism of my family's country and did not want to add to the pile. You mention Nigeria and people generally respond with two associated words, corruption and poverty. It rarely changes, even now.

We had grown up on a diet of poverty porn from Africa,

beamed via the white celebrity saviours on Comic Relief who hugged black babies and demanded that we donate our cash to help save Africa from itself. I didn't want my malaria to contribute to the poor old Africa discussion.

Nigeria has one of the most diverse and successful economies in Africa, yet I'd often hear people casually labelling it as a hopeless third world cesspit. That wasn't the Nigeria I knew. I refused to blame Nigeria; I could have contracted malaria anywhere in the world. I have returned to see my family in Nri several times after my recovery and will continue to do so for many years to come.

In Loughborough, everything was broken down into 50 metres to start with. I started jogging, then worked up to 100, before eventually gingerly completing a full lap of the track. Everything was designed to just test my body a little bit more.

I wanted to know how much my body could take and how far I could push it. I felt far off full strength and speed, but the fact that I had progressed from walking to nearly running was enough hope to sustain me. Everything was against the odds, I was lucky to even be alive, never mind competing for an Olympic spot.

I now felt reinvigorated just being back training with my coach Graham and feeling like an athlete again. I was about to complete my first 400 metre workout under strict instructions to stride the rep, not sprint. It was a cold day, and I would normally opt for the indoor track, but I asked if we could stay outside.

After all the freezing training sets that I had dreaded and endured for years, I was now appreciating every moment and relished feeling the icy air on my skin.

I started running, and immediately was brought back to the joy that I had experienced as a young girl in Wavertree. I wasn't worried about the time; I was running because I finally felt free.

I started to pick up speed at the 200 metre mark, feeling an element of fear about pushing my body too far, but still ignoring Graham's increasingly loud pleas to slow down. I rounded the last turn in the track and even though I was exhausted I knew that I had smashed my own barriers.

I crossed the line in a time of 70 seconds, a full 20 seconds from an Olympic final time, but the toughest race I have ever completed was over and I had won it.

Martyn Rooney was one of very few teammates who knew about my malaria diagnosis and cheered for me loudly as I completed one of the most important laps of my career. "Can you actually imagine Anny after all of this, after everything that you've gone through, if you win an Olympic medal?" he asked when I finished.

The next challenge beckoned, and I couldn't wait to start it.

17

Cheated

THERE ARE few lonelier places in athletics than the call room. It's a place where the clock's hands move slowly and your heart rate quickens. I have been in call rooms all over the world before races and I hate them all. They vary in size and space, but the creeping tension is always there. You sit closely beside competitors, knee to knee. Sometimes there is a stilted polite conversation, but in my case, there is always silence.

One month before the Olympics, I am in Amsterdam, in the last call room before the 400 metres of the European Athletics Championships final. I sit with my head down, refusing to make eye contact with anyone, the only company I have are my anxious thoughts.

My imposter syndrome is looming larger than ever. Will my legs fail me? Have I trained enough? Am I good enough to be here? Can I banish my poor performance in the previous race, and get that last individual spot in the 400? Has the malaria weakened my body or mind beyond repair? My mind is an active one, it always has been. It has the potential to relive memories and soundtracks with the same detail and clarity as a big budget Hollywood film. You want to know the time I ran as a schoolgirl and I will be able to tell you it to two decimal points.

I think back to the final Olympic trials in Birmingham only a few weeks before Amsterdam. In Birmingham, the two fastest women in the final will be automatically selected for Team GB in the 2016 Olympics in Rio de Janeiro, the third and final slot will be at the coach's discretion.

In an Olympic trial anything can and does happen, all bets are off in this race. I always hated the all or nothing pressure of them. For years the trials consumed me with raw anxiety that frequently hampered my performance. You can be running the perfect season, but it all means nothing if you can't deliver at this stage and secure your spot for the Games.

Like the centre forward who stumbles over a penalty kick, it is the cruel all or nothing nature of sport. Single moments that can define your life forever if you let them.

In the final, I take my place in lane six. In a sport full of superstitions and rituals, the sixth lane is a prized spot for most athletes. I hear the starter call 'set', the word I've heard thousands of times, and explode out of the blocks with the sound of the gun. Within 200 metres, almost entering into full acceleration, my mind starts its inner monologue.

"You're off the pace. Far too slow. You're coasting and

you're too far back. You're nowhere near the top two. Why are you so relaxed? Go faster. Get with it now." It's hopeless. My brain is demanding things that my body won't do. I see the clock at the 200 metre mark and see that it's already 25 seconds into the race. That's confirmation that I'm really going far too slow and the race is passing me by.

I'm desperately trying to accelerate and the panic is setting in. I've lost my moment when I should have broken clear of the field and there's far much work to make up. My legs are rusty and mechanical. I can't catch Emily Diamond and Seren Bundy-Davies. I finish third and see my name flash up on the big screen with my slowest time of the year, 52.57 seconds, for the world to see. It simply confirms that my dreams and destiny are now out of my hands.

I collapse in the warmup area, not out of exhaustion, but in despair. Rana is frantically searching for answers for both of us. "What the hell happened out there? That race was over in the first 200 metres. You weren't running your race, you were worried about everyone else." Rana's tone is harsh, but I need to hear it. I choked like I never have before.

This was meant to be an easy job. He then tries to console me, but it's pointless. I'm hysterical. I've now been forced to do a 'race off' in the European Championships. I know that the final spot for the British Olympic team will come between Christine and me. Christine missed the British Championships due to illness, and she is the one person in the world I don't want to face.

Cheated

Christine and I once shared a living room full of laughter in London and now we are opponents, coldly staring at the floor in silence, before the 400 metre European final. Christine is like a sister to me, but the track is a place of business, and today my job is to make sure I beat her. We are held in the call room for an interminable 20 minutes. Just before we head onto the track, Christine softly grabs me by the arm. "Good luck", she says. "Good luck to you too," I reply. I momentarily feel guilty for my detachment, but am buoyed by the raucous Amsterdam crowd as we walk out to our blocks.

I stand at the starting line. I am in the third lane, and just up ahead, in the sixth lane, I can see Christine. The supremely talented Italian runner, Libania Grenot, is in the form of her life, and I know she will be extremely quick over the first 200 metres, alongside the French flyer, Floria Guei.

I had spoken to my psychologist Donovan Pyle in the days before the race, to calm my troubled mind. Bad period pain arrived just before the final, and I am concerned that this is a bad omen on top of my disaster in Birmingham. Donovan has told me to relax and trust in my ability. We both know that it's now or never.

The race starts and, as predicted, Grenot sprints into an early lead. Yet, after 200 metres, my body and mind are working seamlessly together, unlike in Birmingham. My mind is clear and knows that I am running well and my legs have more to give. Even running at almost full pace in front of a screaming crowd, I somehow can go through a logical mental process, 'Have you more to give? Yes. Are the legs ready to do the final push? Absolutely. Let's go.'

I can feel the pressure mounting with every step I take. I know it's going to come down to inches. I consciously close my eyes for the last 15 metres. I know that Christine will be right there beside me. I close my eyes because I cannot bear to look either side of me to see where she is. I dive for the line frantically in darkness. I drop to the floor and Grenot comes over to hug me. I open my eyes. I have come third and beaten Christine, with my best time that year. Christine comes over, and softly says, "You ran a great race, congratulations." It meant everything to hear her say that.

After the elation comes the expectation. I go straight over to Rana and he hugs me. He tells me that he's proud of me. When Rana says it, you know he means it. I ask him if I have done enough to get that last individual spot for the Olympics. He tells me to not worry about it and to just enjoy the moment. I wonder whether he is trying to let me down softly because perhaps he knows something I don't. I put the conspiracy theories aside. I have beaten Christine on one of the biggest stages there is and put in a strong performance in the gold medal winning 4x400 team.

I tell myself to set the worry aside and enjoy the delights of Amsterdam. After hardly touching a drop of alcohol for almost a year, I let the red wine flow to toast a rare personal triumph.

Reality comes on Monday morning in the shape of a 6am EasyJet flight from Amsterdam to Liverpool. The British Olympic athletics team will be selected on Monday and announced to the public on Tuesday, so I want to be at home for the news. I am confident that I have done enough to achieve that final place in the team.

I could not have done any more. I have done well in the final exam, but now I must wait for my results, which unfortunately, cannot be graded purely on the logic that defined my degree in economics.

A bronze medal at the European Championships may not be enough. Christine is a two-time world champion and Olympic gold medallist and there is a slight chance that her reputation may overshadow my European bronze medal.

I decide to wait for the results at my Aunt Bisi's house in Liverpool. Whether the news is good or bad, I want to be in a place of comfort and the best place to be is with Bisi. Whatever I have going on in my life, Bisi knows the perfect way to distract me chatting about anything and everything.

My phone eventually rings, and it is Stephen Maguire, Head of Sprints at British Athletics. He starts off the conversation in that classically polite British way of asking how I have been. We awkwardly dance around the small talk before he finally delivers the news I have been craving for days in his distinctive Northern Irish accent.

"Anyika, this was one of the toughest decisions we faced, especially after your performance in the Europeans," he began. "We have decided to go with Christine for the last spot on the 400 metres team, but we would like you to join the relay team. Honestly, we went back and forward all day, trying to decide, but we've gone with experience and picked Christine."

My disappointment immediately turns to anger. I had done everything they asked me to do and more. He tells me I can appeal the decision in the next 72 hours. I get off the phone and into the arms of Bisi. Bisi is a gifted problem solver, and she had just been landed with the biggest one of my career. Over the next day, her living room was transformed into a legal war room, where we built a large appeal document, covering everything from my results, head to head performances with Christine, to my statement. We submitted the appeal document exhausted.

The appeal was clinical and rigorous in its proposal of my case. The document wasn't a personal attack on Christine, it simply presented black and white facts. Regardless, it wasn't two lawyers locking horns over the minutiae over footnotes in a book of statutes, it was Christine and me. A woman I consider a sister. If I'm successful, she is deselected and I know that every single sentence I have written in my appeal will be given to her to read. Both of us are now in an impossible situation where there can be no winners.

I can't sleep and I'm a mess. Only two days before I was celebrating two medals in the European Championships, now all I can do is wait helplessly. I leave Liverpool on Tuesday morning to return to training in Loughborough, and I'm crying as I get into the car. Through the car window, Mum wipes my tears from my face and softly says, "Bend, don't break." They can twist and turn me, but I tell myself that this won't break me. I know that on the journey I will hear the team announced on the radio.

I am listening to the soothing sound of Frank Ocean's *Sweet Life*, momentarily distracting me from the impending announcement. At 3pm, I switch off Frank and turn on BBC Radio 5 Live to hear the team and sure enough, now the world knows that the final spot in 400 metres has gone to Christine. My phone is frantically pinging with messages and missed calls that I am not in a fit state to answer.

I will hear about my appeal on Friday, but I know that ultimately, it is a pointless exercise. The case that Bisi and I put together will do nothing and they will stick with Christine. UK Athletics will not lose face, regardless of the facts on my appeal. The reality of my situation hits me, and I am hit with a mass of self-loathing. When it mattered most, and I needed to deliver at the trials, I choked spectacularly.

I know I'm in the relay team, but not in the individual 400 metre slot I had worked so tirelessly to achieve. The spot that I wanted so badly for my friends, family and community, to show what was possible through their support. I desperately wanted redemption for what had happened in London.

I will still compete in another Olympic relay team, but honestly, it doesn't matter now. I am unable to process basic logic. My mind is pitch black and I am driving down the A6, hysterically crying. Tears of anger that burn my face as I drive. Anger at the injustice. Rage at having your hopes and dreams ended in a boardroom. Despair at being forced to strain a sisterhood possibly beyond repair.

I am not proud to say this, but at that moment, I wanted to kill myself. Writing this now, I shake when I think that I genuinely considered losing my life over selection for an individual spot to an Olympic Games. Similarly, it didn't make any sense that I had almost killed myself only two years before in the London Olympics over two poor performances in the heats.

I was still going to the Olympics to compete as part of the relay team. Moreover, how could I contemplate ending everything over a race? The problem is when that race is everything that you have worked towards, sacrificing everything – financial security, friends, family and boyfriends – you start to lose perspective, fast. They say that to be a successful athlete, you have to become selfish, and in doing so, your self-worth and *raison d'etre* can become so closely intertwined with your ambitions. I didn't achieve what I set out to do, so I felt utterly worthless, the same as I had felt in London.

The speedometer creeps up to 100 mph. I should only be going at 70, and I don't really care. I hit the accelerator harder, and we go to 130. I have no business going at this speed. The speed of the car reminds me almost of the last

100 metres of the European Championship final, an out of body experience almost, being carried by something else that is far bigger than me. My phone has started to ring incessantly since the news of the team broke, people ringing to console and commiserate. I ignore their calls and keep flooring the accelerator. I have it all worked out, I am going to crash into a wall at high speed and end my life right there.

I momentarily pick up my phone from the floor and for a split second, I feel the car lose control as it swerves manically. I imagine this is what it will be like when I end my life. Out of control, but ultimately quick and painless. I feel a mad shiver of pleasure. I know that I can absolutely die in the next few seconds and wonder which lamppost I want to wrap the car around. The sprinter who died driving her car far too fast.

The car's rev counter is flickering madly, responding to the heavy demands I am putting on the engine. I'm telling myself, do it. Just fucking do it. Somehow, the nightmare finally ends and I calm myself long enough to safely pull over to the hard shoulder and turn off the engine. I can't put my family and friends through a needless death. I am physically heaving with crying and can't see out of my eyes clearly. I pray for this pain to go away.

When I recover enough to drive 20 minutes home, I see a stranger waiting outside my door. I am in no mood for visitors, so I do a large lap around the block. When I return, he is still there.

He is a member of the press looking for comment. I ask

him where he got my address, he refuses to say, so I refuse to speak. I go home, close the door, draw the curtains, and shut out the world completely. It can wait another day.

On Friday, I am back in training in Loughborough and the world is completely oblivious that I came close to moving from the back page of the newspaper, and straight into the obituaries.

The chair of UK Athletics Ed Warner phones me, and starts with polite small talk. I can hear water lapping and music in the background. He eventually breaks the news.

"I know you're waiting to hear an update, well, we've reconvened and looked over your appeal in detail," he said. "We wanted to let you know that we've still gone with Christine. You've been a leader on this team, and I have no doubt you will continue to do an excellent job in Rio."

I demand to know why my form counts for nothing, and Christine's reputation trumped it. I ask what sort of example does that set for any aspiring athlete competing for a place in a British team? Ed tries to calm me by telling me we'll discuss future selection policy in time. I tell him there's absolutely no point. He politely ends the call, telling me that he's got to get back to his holiday in the south of France.

I understand no matter how hard I fight; I will never quite get the better of the boardroom.

My business is on the track, and I am determined to channel this anger into the best performance possible.

18

Rio

EVERYTHING IS heightened in an Olympic year.

It seems that smells are more vivid, sounds are more piercing and the tension is that bit more palpable. Everything as an athlete builds towards the Olympics. Of course World Championships and Commonwealth Games matter a great deal, but this is different. You are not only trying to nail your legacy, but you are also trying to find some sort of financial stability from success. If the athlete succeeds at an Olympics, then so does the coach. Similarly to a stable that produces a Grand National winner, a coach will boast of the achievements of his charges and reap the rewards for years, or even decades to come.

I knew that to operate to the best of my ability, I had to maximise my time with Rana, regardless of the cost, or inconvenience of getting to Holland. I would regularly drive from Loughborough to Essex, board an overnight ferry with the long haul truck drivers and then drive from Rotterdam to the training centre. I knew it was a small sacrifice that would hopefully pay off substantially in the future.

In training, although there was a direct benefit to being in Rana's presence, I increasingly struggled with his erratic moods. One minute he was laughing and full of banter ahead of a session and then, just as suddenly, he would turn moody and sullen. If the Olympics were our final exams, our Professor was increasingly hard to read and wore the tension heavily.

Overthinking is something that I do particularly well. I would regularly worry about whether I have given everything of myself, not only as an athlete, but as a friend and teammate. After nearly dying of malaria and coming close to committing suicide a few weeks prior, my perspective totally changed. I was just grateful to be getting the opportunity to compete in the Olympics. I appreciated every moment as a professional athlete.

Whenever I would have a bad training session or a bad race, I would remember learning how to walk around the corridors of the hospital after my malaria diagnosis. I have never felt more liberated and had no fear of anybody or anything. Once you have nearly experienced death, you start to appreciate the utter fragility of life and just how precious it is. I had no time to waste anymore.

I found joy in running again. When you break down our sport and take it away from the sports scientists and their detailed data reports, it's a fairly straightforward thing. You run from point A to point B in as quick a time as possible. There is a beauty in running and it doesn't matter whether it is kids in a playground or an Olympic stadium, there's a wonderful simplicity to it. There was no need to overthink it, I was finally able to just enjoy it.

I was happy to be training with some of the best athletes in the world, such as the Dutch 200 metre World Champion, Dafne Schippers. The majority of my training group had no clue about my malaria, and it was a point of pride that I never spoke about it. I didn't want any excuses. Going through sprint drills with Dafne on the track was a long way away from shuffling around the hospital with a drip, but it showed what was possible. I was in a daily dog fight training with these athletes and I loved it. It provided the perfect preparation before I stepped onto the plane to travel to Brazil with the British team.

We travelled to our holding camp in the city of Belo Horizonte, surrounded by mountains and hundreds of miles inland from the Games in Rio de Janiero. The holding camp is where athletes go to fine tune everything ahead of major championships like the Olympics and World Championships. You are far from distractions and I normally loved them.

After years of struggling to pay the bills, and rushing across the world to compete, you finally felt that you had made it. You were lifted and laid for ten days, with all your laundry and cooking done for you. All that you have to do is worry about ensuring that you are ready to compete in the Olympics.

At holding camps, I enjoyed getting to know new teammates from every possible event in track and field. Even though my sport is an individual one, it can still be extremely cliquey. I never cared about that, I would sit with anyone and chat to them.

I loved to hear their insights on their event, and what gave them the edge, be it in the marathon or the javelin. Everybody has a story and I want to hear them. For instance, as a rule, distance runners were quiet and introspective, and never sat with sprinters who tended to be boisterous and loud. I always insisted on sharing a room with a distance runner as it meant that you were able to go to bed nice and early in perfect silence.

One thing I consistently noticed at British Olympic holding camps was the subtle colour divide in the dining room. There would generally be a large group of black athletes sitting together, and another of white athletes on the long tables in the dining area. This can be easily explained that sprint events generally have a high amount of black athletes, and conversely distance events are filled with white athletes.

I remember seeing a packed dining room and a small female white distance runner had nowhere to sit, you could see her eyes darting around the room almost in a panic. Immediately the group of black sprinters made room for her and beckoned her over to sit. She sat down, and I immediately noticed them change their behaviour. Their raucous banter died down and they quickly and seamlessly adapted to make her feel more comfortable.

This colour delineation was never deliberate at holding camps, but it was noticeable. I still wonder why did these black sprinters feel that they had to be quieter to welcome a solitary white woman? She had put them under no pressure to do so, yet they felt compelled by an unspoken rule that we all had to adapt to make others feel comfortable so they didn't feel threatened? I did it myself for so many years on and off the track. I was worried that I'd be too loud, too outspoken, or even too aggressive as a black woman. I would adapt my behaviour to fulfil an unspoken societal rule that I had to adapt to make others feel comfortable. Thankfully, those days are long gone. I refuse to dilute my personality to appease societal diktats I never agreed to in the first place.

While I normally enjoyed the Olympic holding camp experience; Belo Horizonte could be best described as purgatory with beige food. We sat in a state of almost constant tension, breaking the tedium by eating from a menu that has been designed to fit the bland culinary specifications of our sports scientists. There was no seasoning of any description used in the dry food and we were tormented by the smells from a Brazilian barbecue restaurant downstairs where the coaching staff would feast every night, while the athletes sullenly chewed on brown rice and broccoli upstairs.

When you grow up in a Caribbean or an African household, as many of the British team did, seasoning is what brings your food to life and I found that I was suffering serious withdrawal symptoms. One night, I sneaked out to TGI Fridays, under the cover of darkness, with my coach Graham and demolished a steak and a small glass of red wine. I would never normally indulge before a championship, but, after a week of drab dinners, I enjoyed every morsel.

Our late night escape was almost foiled when we got into the wrong Uber and found ourselves lost, in the middle of a huge favela, reminiscent of the Brazilian film *City of God*. Thankfully, through a combination of broken English and Portuguese, we got back to camp safe and sound.

Since my appeal against Christine's selection ahead of me on the team, we had barely spoken, beyond a polite 'hello' in the corridor or some words at relay practice. Her room in camp was opposite to mine, and while we were always going to be extremely professional, undoubtedly at this Olympics our relationship had changed. I found it tough to adapt to this new divide between us that hadn't been of our making. I would have loved nothing more than to have called into her room like the old days and chatted for hours.

For years, Christine had been that beacon of calmness and solace for me and a connection with my early years. Now I felt I had lost her forever.

While I missed having her friendship, I also knew that she might not want to speak to me after everything that had happened during the appeals process. It wasn't just about me and what I wanted from her, I had a responsibility to ensure that Chrisine didn't have any distractions that could hinder her performance. I still strongly believed that I had done everything to earn the individual spot in the 400 metres which had gone to her, but that is sport and life, and both of us had to move on.

When you finally leave the holding camp, it is as if a weight has been lifted off your shoulders. The Olympics are within touching distance, and everything that you have worked for is going to be put to the test. I always try to take a window seat on a plane, as it allows you to work out the place that you are going from the best vantage point.

Flying into Lagos, I often look down at the fields, and the teeming city streets filled with busy professionals and wonder what is happening in their lives. In Rio, I looked at the huge Christ the Redeemer statue and the glistening blue sea below and wondered what the people below would make of this Olympics. I couldn't wait to find out.

After I arrived at the Olympic Village it suddenly all became very real. This was my third Olympics, and I was used to its peculiar rhythm and energy, but it still daunted me. It can feel like the first day of school, with confident athletes strutting around in peak physical condition.

You try not to steal glances at your competitors, but you might catch a snippet of their training session and see that they're running extremely fast. Ultimately, the Olympics is as much a mental test as a physical one.

On the day of team selection, I sat there with the same

nerves that I had felt in my first Olympics. You're there with some of your closest friends and competitors, all vying for four slots on a relay team, that will ultimately define your destiny as an athlete. We knew that after the superpowers of the USA and Jamaica, on our day, we could easily ward off the challenge of Ukraine, Canada and France.

I looked around the room and found no clues in anyone's faces. Ross Tugwood, the team's sport scientist, started giving a presentation on our performances as individual athletes in cold, hard, data. This entrée is generally hard to swallow, but I managed to stomach it. I knew that I had run as well as any girl competing in the relay. Then it was left up to Stephen Maguire to announce the final team.

"It's never easy to deliver this news, we know how much you've all put into it," he started. "We've obviously taken into account your performances, but not only that, we have been watching people in the holding camp and in the village to see that they are on the job. Here's the team for the first heat, in order of legs, Emily Diamond, Anyika Onuora, Kelly Massey and Christine Ohuruogu."

I never took anything for granted, no matter how well I was running, and was delighted to hear my name. There was instant relief. You can't celebrate in that moment; you must be sensitive to the other athletes in the room. I was that athlete in Beijing who was left disappointed and watching from the stands.

Stephen reminded the athletes who weren't picked for the

heat that they still had a job to do in training and the team for the final wasn't selected yet.

I got out of the room and met Rana. He was pleased, but in business mode. "Well done, but it's time to get ready to roll; I'll see you on the track tonight." After years of tension about competing, now that the moment had come in Rio, I was completely relaxed.

The pain of the journey to get here had made my arrival so much more pleasant. I was entering into such an untypical zen state that I was drifting into sleep as we arrived at the stadium and Christine nudged me, looking concerned, after seeing me in a ball of nervous tension at so many events over the years. "Are you alright Anyika?" she asked. "Never better Christine, never better." I smiled. It was go time.

We qualified into the final, coming second in our heat behind the Jamaicans. I had run well and was relieved to be picked for the final with Eilidh Doyle replacing Kelly. I arrived at the track and immediately set into my normal routine. I walked into the warmup area and tried not to make any eye contact with anyone, whether it was a teammate or a competitor. I tried to avoid any distraction whatsoever. Music has always given me strength and solace, at the best and worst times in my life.

At the start of my warmup, I'd have some gospel music, then progress to Nirvana's *Smells Like Teen Spirit* before reaching the crescendo with some rap pulsing through my headphones. The lyrics of the rapper Meek Mill's *Dreams and Nightmares* were etched in my brain as the final song before I'd compete.

I bounced on the soles of my shoes and rolled my shoulders like a boxer about to go into a title fight. Meek Mill rapped:

> *Ain't this what they've been waiting for?*
> *You ready?*
> *I used to pray for times like this, to rhyme like this*
> *So I had to grind like that to shine like this*

We walk into a team huddle on the grass by the track and run through some final instructions. We link arms, and you understand that, in this moment, you will give everything for these women, and they will do exactly the same for you. I am trying to focus in on what is being said when I'm distracted by a senior UK Athletics official speaking rapidly.

"I hope these girls are fucking ready. There's 10 million quid in funding on the line if they don't get a medal. I'm telling you they better fucking get this together tonight."

I wasn't meant to hear these words, and I'm still not sure if any of the other girls heard them. It's impersonal, callous and says everything about the individual. It underscores that this is not a collection of women that have sacrificed almost everything to represent their country, instead, we provide an opportunity to underline the final financial report and keep UK Athletics out of the red for another four years. I wish I could say that I was surprised, but after over a decade in the system, it is to be expected.

I walk into the call room and catch Rana's eye, he beckons me over. "You better not leave this stadium without a medal," he said. "This is what you've worked for, all those days and nights; remember your steps, remember to stay relaxed, you're in great shape, let's go do this Anny, now get to work." I just nod.

Before or since, I have never felt so much confidence before a race. It had become more than a race for me, it had become the symbol of something bigger. I should have been dead, either from malaria or suicide. I was repeatedly sexually assaulted in the system. My hair, body and skin colour were under constant scrutiny. I had been viciously racially abused. I had come back from it all and was standing tall in the call room, ready to enter the Olympic stadium.

I lie on the ground of the first call room, with my legs splayed to stop them cramping up. I don't want to talk to anyone. We are sharing a room with Canada, and true to their national stereotype, they are achingly polite. "Oh sorry, I'm sitting a bit close to you," "I just wanted to wish you the very best of luck ahead of the race," "Have you enjoyed the Olympics so far?"

In terms of reverse psychology, it would be a masterstroke, but the truth is, they are just very nice people with no ulterior motive. I try to stay in the zone and retain my energy, finding solace in Christine's complete calmness, as she cracks jokes as if she was waiting for a bus, not an Olympic final.

We are then summoned into the second call room. This is when it becomes even more real. The tension has increased, even the polite Canadians are stunned into silence. The wait in the call room is often unbearable, you can sit in them for five or 30 minutes at a time, with nothing to distract you.

From the second call room, you can often hear the sound of the crowd rising from the stadium outside and the stamping of feet. The official comes into the room and calmly says, "Ladies, it's time to get ready."

I walk out into the stadium, and my first reaction was *wow, the Brazilian fans could have at least filled the stadium!* We had been spoiled by the pandemonium of the packed crowds in London four years before. It didn't matter, I could still see the British flags waving in the stadium and the noise started to build as we walked out to the track. My heart starts really thumping and I start to recite Psalm 23:

> *Even though I walk*
> *through the darkest valley,*
> *I will fear no evil,*
> *for you are with me;*
> *your rod and your staff,*
> *They comfort me.*

I know that I will relive this race in my dreams forever.

The gun goes off and Eilidh Doyle runs the first leg and

I stand helplessly waiting for her. No matter how well she is running, she seems to be further and further away. Whether it's to control my anxiety and breathing I am not sure, but I have developed a weird habit of always swirling water in my mouth just before the baton comes, and then quickly spitting it out. I finally see Eilidh coming, spit the water out and explode off my mark. We are in fifth place and have to make up considerable ground.

Curiously, I am completely calm, and almost enjoying the race. I focus on my steps and breathing. Everything is in sync. I increase my speed and pass Canada and Poland. I am now chasing the USA and Jamaica. I am telling myself, just stay calm. Please stay calm and relax. Like I am trying to get my stubborn inner-child to focus on the job at hand. I am running well, probably as well as I have ever run in my career, but I fear the crippling monster that is lactic acid – it can burn every tendon in your legs and render them useless in seconds if you are not careful.

I enter the final 100 metres, and suddenly the monster looms out of the shadows and starts spewing lactic all over my body. I can barely breathe as my lungs become restricted and I am now running through thick quick-sand.

I see Emily Diamond on the horizon, she can't be more than 40 metres away, but she might as well be on the other side of Brazil. My legs are losing traction as she frantically screams at me to keep going. She's bouncing up and down as I was only a minute earlier, desperate to take on the baton. I have burnt way too much energy chasing down Poland and Canada and I can feel them breathing down my neck, pulling me back. It feels like this moment that I've been waiting for my whole life is now about to escape me. I lurch forward and finally; I give Emily the baton.

I refuse to look at the screen. My first reaction is I ran badly and went out far too quickly. I brought us back to third place, but in the last desperate seconds of my leg we fell to sixth as the lactic burnt my legs to oblivion.

The race is out of my hands.

In the third leg, Emily runs the race of her life to restore us to third place, and hands the baton to Christine. I can still barely look, but I'm screaming for her. The roar of the crowd tells me that the race is tight.

Christine is holding third place, but she has a pack following her closely as she moves into the final straight fighting for the third place on the podium behind Jamaica and the United States who are engaged in their own fight for gold.

Allyson Felix crosses in first place, I see the Americans celebrating, then Novlene Williams-Mills of Jamaica in silver. I allow myself to gaze through my fingers, Christine looks utterly relaxed and with a final burst crosses in third.

I have finally won an Olympic medal.

I almost collapse in the sheer joy and elation of the moment. I am not fully in control of my body or my emotions. I am screaming and crying. I want to live in this moment forever. Cameras are flashing all around me and I am almost blinded by them.

My mind then starts to slowly collate where I am, it is fighting against too much stimulation. Slowly, in the ecstasy of this moment, I think back to Mum and Dad and life in Liverpool. Standing proudly with sports-day medals with Mum and nestled beside Dad watching Britain win Olympic medals in Sydney. Now it is my turn. I did it for them.

The team hug and I envelope Christine. Years of financial sacrifice, lonely nights, torn inside from sexual assault, facing death too many times, and suddenly, your dream comes true. We do the lap of honour, something that I watched friends like Jess Ennis-Hill do for years at Olympics, and always wondered what it would be like.

We see the cheering British crowd and calling our names. Flags are thrown down to us. Now I know, I do not want the moment to end. You walk around the stadium, trying to slow your footsteps and enjoy every bit of this moment.

I think of my family and community, sitting at home in Liverpool and Nri watching on the TV, roaring me across the finish line. I think of my Dad who would have given anything to be in the stadium right now and I know that Mum is ringing every relative in Nigeria to let them know that her daughter is an Olympic medallist.

My aunties will be cooking up a celebratory feast in Liverpool, and glasses of stout and palm wine will be toasted late into the night in Nri.

We eventually leave the track and go back to the warmup track. Steven and Neil give us all a huge hug that reminds me of the official in the moments before we went out and raced. This race wasn't just about four women winning a medal, it has saved the collective asses of UK Athletics officialdom. They have hit their targets and their hugs are filled with sheer relief.

I find a moment in my bedroom when we finally get back to the Olympic Village and look at the medal in my hand. I go to the shower and cry as I don't want to wake up Shara. Finally, with the hot water running all over my body, I shed tears of joy.

It's a funny feeling, almost like getting the Christmas present that you had always wanted, and now it's finally unwrapped and yours to keep forever. Ultimately, the final was far bigger than any medal or even any notion of the Olympic dream. So many times I had asked myself why I had continued in this sport.

Finally I knew why.

19

Last Legs

I REGULARLY speak to former Olympians from a variety of sports about their experiences after the Games, medal winner or not, and the answers are always different.

Some feel a devastating anticlimax; they have climbed a dangerous summit for many years, to ultimately find there was nothing there at the top. For others, the Olympics can change their life, launch a media career or catapult them up the corporate ladder. The majority of athletes just quietly move on, immediately forgotten after the packed victory parades and only remembered in a random pub quiz question or in their parents' scrapbook.

When we finally arrived back home, I allowed myself to enjoy the victory parade, waving to the cheering crowd in London. It is a curious feeling, in your Olympic tracksuit, with the Games still fresh in people's mind, you're almost like Wonder Woman putting on her cape, everyone wants to be in your presence, and you politely smile for every selfie. After being at three Games, I knew a week later that I would be back in Loughborough doing my weekly shop in Sainsbury's, completely anonymous.

After Rio, I returned home exhausted. My body and mind were drained. I knew that I was getting older, and it was getting increasingly harder. I'd wake up, and I'd feel my calves, achilles and knees ache badly. I'd have to complete a pseudo judo roll to get out of bed, and then I'd not be able to walk properly. I'd tip toe, hoping that these tiny steps would help to reduce the strain on my battered body.

In spite of the increasing niggles, I was still determined to get to Tokyo for my final Olympics. I knew that I would be 35 and would have a battle not only against the stopwatch, but against my body. It didn't matter. After winning bronze in Rio, I knew that when I put my mind to it, anything was possible. After so many years of my career not going right, I finally felt that I had found my rhythm.

Waiting for the flight home from Rio de Janeiro, I sat happily chatting to teammates, when I saw the attempted rapist awkwardly weave his way down through the departure lounge, stumbling as he went, the stench of alcohol coming from every pore on his body. He was en route to the duty free to stock up on more cheap booze. The flashbacks immediately returned and I was lost in a mental tailspin that I could not stop. I didn't join in with the laughter, staring down at the tiled floor until he passed.

I boarded the plane held in a tight grip of panic and fear.

I had been so happy and now in an instant he had ruined it. I sat beside the 800 metre runner Shelayna Oskan-Clarke and held onto her. She must have thought that I was a nervous flyer, with no idea about the truth. I knew that I didn't want to see him, if I did I was going to break down in the toilet. I got the thin airline blanket, threw it over my head and took frequent deep breaths to get through the journey home.

The panic attacks triggered by the attempted rape could come at any moment, and often with no warning. Every year, I spent hours on a detailed schedule for the year, to ensure that when possible, I had little to do with him and our paths would not cross.

He had tried to ruin my life, but I wouldn't let him take my livelihood and what I loved. Every time I saw him I wanted to crumble and cry, but I simply compartmentalised the trauma.

Most athletes are guilty of living in the moment simply because we have no choice. We live from race to race, and strategically peak as the major championships arrive. The sensible work of planning a career after athletics seldom happens, you are just concentrating on enjoying this merry-go-round that you do not want to get off.

The problem is, it's not your decision whether you continue as a professional athlete, and that is hard to confront. The stopwatch and your body will let you know that it is time to exit the arena long before you can contemplate making that decision yourself.

How does any athlete know when the perfect time to stop is? The majority don't – even an idol like Muhammad Ali was getting viciously beaten up by men in his last fights who couldn't have lived with him in his prime.

I remember Ali once said that his mind stayed clear in his last bouts, but his body just wouldn't follow what his brain had commanded it to do. Like the once, blindingly fast, Ali shuffle fading with age, I was going to have to confront my own suddenly senior status in the sport, whether I wanted to or not.

After I had heard the UK Athletics official bark that if our relay team didn't win a medal in Rio, we would be burning 10 million pounds in funding, I started to think about my own financial future in more detail. I had no safety net to provide a comfortable landing, either in the form of a pension, or an investment portfolio.

The roar of the crowd in Rio and the ecstasy of the victory parade in London were long forgotten by the time I had my end-of-season chat with Stephen Maguire in September 2017, where, amongst other things, my funding would be discussed.

I got used to these discussions with Stephen. They were like every dull corporate performance review you can imagine, except, instead of sales figures, our race times were held on a piece of printed A4 and pored over with a microscope.

A split second gained in Stockholm or lost in London could define your future. There were never bonuses on the line, simply the promise of the basic lifeline of funding, or getting your safety harness stripped away mid-flight.

There was a brief preamble from Stephen, about my form throughout 2017, that hadn't been brilliant, not helped by a hamstring injury and the missed drug tests, but equally did show moments of promise. I tried to focus on what he was saying. "Anyika, you've been a great leader in this team for many years, and your contribution has been magnificent. Your dedication to this cause can never be faulted. We do have concerns however. You're travelling back and forward to Holland to see Rana and we think this is affecting your form."

My response was direct, but I had no choice. "I have been travelling up and down the country, and sleeping on ferries, to get proper training with my coach in Holland," I explained. "There has been no choice here, it's all I could do. You got rid of him, but gave me no support in finding a suitable alternative. Honestly Stephen, I've been fighting to keep my career going and I've had absolutely no backing from any of you in making it work."

He nodded, not able to come up with an adequate response. He then proceeded to discuss other athletes he wasn't happy with, while I sat there in silence, acting as an unwilling and unpaid therapist. Finally, he told me that he would update me on my funding in due course.

Two months later, I got my answer. UK Athletics were taking me off funding as they didn't think that I was able to make a sufficient contribution to any future team. I had been there before, once you are off funding, then you are in a dog fight to keep your existence as an athlete alive. I knew that the work from me and other athletes over the years had kept people in jobs at UK Athletics, but ultimately, the decision makers don't deal in loyalty, they deal in perceived medal potential.

It felt like it went back to my parents telling me as a young black girl in Britain that I couldn't just be good, I had to be the best at everything I did, and even then, I was to discover that it wasn't enough. In an industry like athletics, they are not only selling the dream of medals and the perfect body, they are selling iconic imagery to their sponsors. Do sporting brands want track and field dominated by black women on the podium at every World Championships and Olympics? Are these athletes going to sell the volume of products that they need? Only they can answer that question.

After my fight to get black female athletes recognised with something as simple as a few posters in the UK Athletics high performance centre, I understood that you had to fight for everything you got with the last breath of effort, on and off the track.

After an unsuccessful appeal to reverse UK Athletics' funding decision, driven once again by my tireless Aunt Bisi, I was hovering on the outside of the inner sanctum of my sport.

In clipped prose, the unilateral conviction of the selection panel was that I was too old to contribute in Tokyo, and in spite of mentoring athletes for years, it was time for me to exit the stage forever.

Slowly, but surely, I became aware of my diminishing value as an athlete, not only by the large electric screens that flashed times that were a second slower than my peak, but from the reaction of competitors, who I had once smoked and were now regularly beating me to the finish line.

Rana became icily cold towards me. I was once a valuable asset who achieved my zenith in 2016 but I was now seemingly entering a long, slow decline. A few months after I had returned from winning bronze in Rio, Rana had contacted me regarding a bonus. It was never written into the contract, as I was fighting to pay our agreed rate as it was.

His pitch was simple. "I know it's not written into the contract, but I'm expecting a bonus," he started. "Remember Anny, I'm not a charity case. I contributed to your most successful season yet." I paid him the bonus, I felt that I had no choice.

Barely a year later, my purpose had been served for Rana. He was ready to get rid of me as soon as possible to focus on his latest prized stocks. It became clear, in the rare training sessions that I could attend in Holland, that I wasn't welcome in his training group anymore, but he didn't tell me directly.

Instead, I dealt with his passive aggression and mood swings. I was still paying him to coach me and he was left with an older athlete running slower times. Ultimately, coaching me was not going to help his career any further, whether financially, or reputationally. My membership in the Tumbleweed Track Club was quickly coming up for renewal.

He always used to say jokingly that whenever an athlete left him, they would lose their speed, almost like Superman being weakened by kryptonite. Unfortunately, you started to believe what he was saying, and I stayed in this awkward partnership that was increasingly denting my self-esteem and bank balance as the 2018 season continued.

It was a relationship that was no longer functioning, but equally I felt that I had little choice but to try and keep the dwindling flame of my athletics career going. I had nowhere else to go. I didn't have the strength to leave Rana, especially at my age.

I rolled back the years to win a bronze medal as part of the 4x400 relay team in the European Championships in Berlin. I wished that I had known that this was the last dance, then I might have stopped to enjoy it more and savour the moment. Germany is one of the best places to compete as an athlete, simply because of the passion of the fans.

They have an encyclopedic knowledge of the athletes competing across every event, and will always make noise in packed stadiums.

My head was in a weird place in Berlin. I had under-performed in the individual 400 metres, getting knocked out in Heat 2 and was surprised to be picked for the final of the 4x400.

On paper I was still the second quickest British athlete over a quarter mile, even if I didn't necessarily feel it at times.

I was competing with Zoey Clarke, Amy Allcock and Eildh Doyle. Girls that I knew and respected, but I missed the familiar comfort that competing with Christine had brought me for so many years on relay teams. There wasn't the same warmth or banter. It felt that it was just about business out there on the track.

I knew that slowly but surely I was getting pushed out of British Athletics. Once you are out of the funding cycle, particularly as a veteran athlete, you are almost always fighting a losing battle. To even be here competing in a major final was a small victory. We walked out to a stadium that was filled with German flags, and fans who gracefully cheered for every nation when the team was announced.

I ran a strong leg, as the second runner, taking the baton from Zoey, before giving it to Amy. I was calm and strong over 350 metres, and then the effort of fending off a triple challenge from Germany, Poland and France became too much.

I saw Amy's hand ready for the baton, and my arms and head are wildly flowing, almost like Eric Liddell in the film *Chariots of Fire*. I can barely breathe or summon the strength to raise my arm to give her the baton. Somehow I do in third place.

Amy then passed it to Eilidh who ran brilliantly to hold off a brave challenge from Belgium's Hanne Claes in a close sprint to the line to secure bronze for Britain. Eildh was crouched exhausted as we slowly came up to her in a huddle. The achievement was a great one, and I was so happy to win another major medal, but there was no raucous celebration or tears from any of us. There was just quiet satisfaction of a job executed well.

Shortly after our race, I overheard one of the boys in the British 4x400 relay team who had won a silver medal 20 minutes before us saying, "Happy days, that's my funding sorted for the next few years." I was disgusted. I knew that even with this medal, I had no hope of getting funding, while some people basked in doing the absolute bare minimum effort.

This statement highlighted the privilege and entitlement of the minority of athletes within the British system. There were those of us who fought for every crumb that fell from the table, and those that gluttonously devoured the spoils of funding off silver platters.

After Berlin, I knew that my relationship with Rana was over. He was leaving Holland to take up a coaching opportunity in Jacksonville, Florida. There was nowhere else to go for either of us. We finally sat down like a married couple that haven't spoken over the dinner table for ten years, the tension broken only by the crackle of the television.

We eventually got down to talking about parting ways. "Do you want to coach me anymore?" I asked, knowing the answer. "I don't think I can coach you," he replied simply. We both hugged, relieved that this relationship was finally over.

I left Holland for the last time, and the American gospel group Mary Mary's song *Shackles (Praise You)* came through the tinny speaker of my car, as I drove through the grey sleepy suburban streets to the ferry in Rotterdam:

Take the shackles off my feet so I can dance
I just wanna praise you
I just wanna praise you
You broke the chains now I can lift my hands
And I'm gonna praise you
I'm gonna praise you

I hardly saw Rana again and the shackles were well and truly off in our tumultuous relationship. I could still put my body through his toughest training assignments, but mentally I knew that I had nothing left to give him. He was a man who had challenged me, infuriated me, but ultimately gave me the greatest gift possible, fulfilling and exceeding my potential as an athlete.

Despite results that told a different story, I still knew that I could compete in the Tokyo Olympics in 2020. I switched to a Swedish coach, Benke Blomkvist, who was a complete cultural shock from the ups and downs of life with Rana.

Where I once sent several panicked Sunday night emails demanding workouts from Rana, I was now enjoying crafted and calm Swedish organisation. Each workout had a purpose and I felt like I had joined a new school, where I missed my old mates badly, but was enjoying the new curriculum a lot more. I was back living full time in Loughborough as I tried to resuscitate my career into producing one last heroic act in Japan.

Although my body was getting stronger, my mind was still prone to stumbling. I was tormented by panic attacks that arrived as soon as I saw the man who had tried to rape me. The moment I saw him, I would feel my heart pound through my chest like a jackhammer. I'd tell myself to keep breathing, to please keep calm. If there was time, I would sprint to the toilet, and control my breathing. If not, I would keep my head down, and pretend to play on my phone.

Anytime that I would see him, it would completely destroy my training routine. I was expected to deliver immaculate performances while a man who had tried to rape me stood close by.

Still, nobody knew a thing. I was desperate to tell anyone, but I couldn't. I would keep it together in the training complex, and when I returned to my house, I would break down in tears. There was too much trauma, and it had been bubbling furiously under the surface for far too many years. I was ready to explode.

In Tenerife for warm weather training in January, and exhausted after a hard session, I turned on my phone to see a group message between Tiffany and Shara. The girls were talking about a new documentary *Surviving R Kelly*, saying that I had to watch it. I watched the first episode, and I knew that I had opened a box of mental pain that I wouldn't have the strength to close. I wanted to stop watching the series, but I was powerless. I had to complete it.

The series was focused on a historical alleged sexual abuse from the RnB singer R Kelly, centred on the stories of African American women, as they fought for justice. One of the victim's words echoed across my apartment, "Black women do not get the same recognition as our white counterparts."

The sickening sexual assaults that Kelly performed on these black women had been forced into the small print of the newspapers, if they had even seen the light of day. If Kelly had held white women against their will in his Atlanta property and performed sex acts on them against their will, would the world have been silent for so long?

The women's accounts of sexual assault broke me. Not only because of the horrifying and graphic nature of their helplessness against a man more powerful financially and physically than them; but how Kelly was protected systemically. He abused the women, but there were people within his entourage that knew exactly what was going on, yet chose to say nothing. Sometimes, the silence is what hurts the most.

I could barely train in Tenerife. The R Kelly series tormented me. It heightened my mental pain and I was unable to fight against it. I couldn't sleep, and my eczema had flared up into fiery red rashes that gave a physical indication of my mental state. I was in a fit of depression, and the burden I was carrying was growing too heavy to hold any longer.

My fight to the Olympic podium against the odds in 2016 had largely acted as a soothing balm for my mental pain, but it was looking increasingly unlikely that I was going to be able to repeat this trick again.

It was a documentary about black women, abused in Atlanta, not where I was, yet I shared their pain. Nobody had believed them, so who the hell was going to believe me? I shared the pain of millions of other women who feel powerless and helpless to rise up and tell their truth.

In May 2019 I travelled to Yokohama to compete in the World Relays and barely slept. I'd look at my roommate Ashleigh Nelson sleeping peacefully, and I'd desperately envy her. I'd go into the bathroom and relive the nightmare that I couldn't shake and break down, sobbing quietly.

In this hotel, I was cornered at every turn. I couldn't escape him. I went to the shop to buy a snack, and when I went to call the lift back to my floor there he was. Just the two of us. He innocently asked me, "Are you going up?". I immediately sprinted out of the hotel and cried, before climbing 20 flights of stairs to my room. I knew that I couldn't control anything anymore, once again there was no escape.

I should have been focused on my race in one of my favourite countries, but I was unable to think clearly. My training sessions were terrible. I was so tense that it was impossible to relax, never mind compete. I smelt the stench of him and booze even when they weren't there and I found it impossible to eat anything.

My mind had moved from competition into purely survival mode. I sat down for breakfast with my teammates, and in the crowded dining room of the hotel space, there were few free seats left. I was lost in my own world, staring at my plate and trying to make polite conversation, when I saw him make his way to our table.

Normally, I would be polite and professional, but now my ability at keeping up appearances had stopped. I was on the verge of exploding at any moment. I threw him a look and told him coldly that it wasn't my problem that he could not find a place to sit. The pretence of politeness was over.

He eventually sat down on our table, but away from me. I genuinely thought of ways of killing him. I went through a list of ways that I could make this happen. Maybe I could stab him with a knife, or even a fork. I saw his hand, and fantasised driving the cutlery through his skin and bone, making him hurt even for a fraction of a second.

After years of my pain, he would finally have a tiny inkling of what it felt like. The problem was in this Japanese hotel there was only wooden cutlery. I sat there desperate and helpless.

My legs had started to feel heavy and unable to generate the power they once used to. When you are reliant on your body to earn your living, you notice its quirks better than any sports scientist can extrapolate from their spreadsheets. I had run 54.8 split in the relay in Yokohama, far slower than my normal pace, leading to Rana sending me a text of genuine concern, asking me if I was ok. He couldn't reconcile the fearless Olympic athlete in Rio, with the runner who looked like her legs were getting pulled back by ropes as she ran. That race was a surprise to every single person apart from me.

Benke remained a wonderful and caring coach, but he knew nothing about my trauma. We tried everything; supplements, changing my training plan, blood tests, more rest, but nothing worked. I was suffering from increasing panic attacks particularly in hotels, and my ability to control things was almost at an end. We were doing a standard 400 metres workout. I took off as normal but I could feel that my body was breaking down at 250 metres, and rendered almost useless. It was like driving a car that was slowly losing power against its will.

I tried to fight my mind and then my body, but I broke down 20 metres short of the finish line. I had never stopped in a training session in my life. I knew something was seriously wrong, and it wasn't going to get better.

As athletes, unfortunately we live and die by times. We're defined by them in the end. Times to be at airports, hotels and stadiums. Times that need to be beaten, or else you are finished. Caroline's phone that had once been busy with invites from race directors all over the world for me had almost gone dead. She was having to call in favours all over Europe to get me a lane and I was embarrassed that I was putting her through this. I was travelling all over Europe as a jobbing athlete, losing money, because I wasn't running quickly enough.

When you are at the end of your career, you start to see your friendships in a clearer light. The people who you had spent days and weeks with at World Championships and Olympics who now studiously ignore you as your star descends; perhaps concerned that a loss of form and getting older is contagious.

I knew that I had to let Tokyo go, it was a dream, but it wasn't going to be mine anymore. I had to let go of my identity as an athlete that had brought me so much joy, but also nearly cost my life.

I was ticking over in training, more out of routine than a competitive urge. I hadn't told anyone that I had officially retired, but in my mind I was no longer an athlete. My friend and former training partner Danielle had once told me that when you are ready to retire, it's just something you know when it comes.

Eventually, I was training with a friend one day when he asked, "Are you ready?" I thought that he meant ready to retire, when he actually meant to start the session. I smiled and said, "Yes, I'm ready." I felt a light breeze that filled my body with peace and calm. Every single set that we did, I embraced every moment, knowing that I was taking my final steps in my career. I completed the session and left the track, knowing that my career as a competitive athlete was over.

Danielle had been right, the time had come and I knew it.

I sat in my house and cried. Long heaving cries that signalled the end of a life that I couldn't have imagined as a little girl growing up in Liverpool.

I had competed in three Olympics, winning a medal in one, alongside the Commonwealth Games, European and World Championships. I asked myself was I happy? I wasn't sure. I wore the wicked wounds of my career in my mind, and they would be far harder to shake off than any physical injury that I carried.

When you finish as an athlete, the phone stops ringing and there is no safety net to catch you. I was a three-time Olympian, but almost institutionalised by the life that I had led for so many years, unsure of how to cope outside the structured confines of sport.

I wasn't sure how I was going to navigate the next stage of my life, but I didn't have a choice. In that moment, I wanted to have nothing to do with athletics. I had given my body, mind and life to it for enough years. I had spent too many years being defined by a stopwatch. I had missed so many normal things.

I wanted to enjoy what life could offer on the other side. Whether that was eating too much at brunch, standing on my feet at a concert or attending the Notting Hill Carnival.

I was looking forward to making up for lost time.

20

Healing

I AM exhausted and drained.

I haven't laced up a pair of running spikes since the end of 2019, but I haven't felt sustained pain like it. The physical pain I can largely deal with, it was a key part of my job for nearly two decades.

I look over my body now, run my fingers over my legs and feel the sinew of each pounded tendon that eventually carried me to more medals than I could have ever dreamt of winning. That pain is manageable, the pain in my heart is not.

When I walked away from professional sport, I barely gave athletics a backwards glance, beyond the odd piece of media work and little bits of coaching to give back to the next generation. My mind was filled with possibilities of life after sport.

Unlike so many athletes I've known who sadly ended their careers in debt financially, or filled with despair about the future, I embraced the uncertainty and held it tight.

My life would no longer be dictated by a detailed timetable of data reports and diet plans. I could finally do whatever I wanted, and I couldn't wait to try.

Whether it was researching further study in economics or exploring my love of fashion, music festivals, film and art, I had so many interests beyond athletics that I wanted to investigate and took full advantage of the opportunity to do so. I was never defined by athletics, even as an Olympian, and as the months passed, I felt its grip on my life loosen gradually which suited me down to the ground.

Like everyone, COVID-19 quickly stopped me in my tracks. In May 2020, I was locked down at home and was dragged back into the world of athletics against my will.

The murder of George Floyd, on an anonymous street in Minneapolis, through the sharp and unrelenting knee of police officer Derek Chauvin, sent shockwaves around the world through the Black Lives Matter movement and reverberated deep into the recesses of sport.

The murder of George Floyd was tragic and brutal, alongside the needless killings in the United States of Breonna Taylor and Ahmaud Arbery a few months apart, but for me and my black teammates, it was like watching a sick and twisted film where we already knew how the final scene would progress.

We have seen this played out before numerous times and we have lived with this trauma our whole lives.

Sitting at home, I started to field countless phone calls and text messages from distressed and traumatised black teammates, who in many cases were unable to compete, let alone train.

The Black Lives Matter movement and the murders of George, Ahmaud and Breonna had brought their own personal traumas to the surface, and they held us all in a vice like grip, refusing to let us free.

There was a clawing pain in many of their voices, memories that had been suppressed for years were finally rising to the surface, and my teammates needed to share their pain. You might have seen these friends of mine on television, competing against the best in the world, and, in many cases, winning major medals for Great Britain. But, when the stadium lights were off, and they were left needing support in light of the Black Lives Matter movement, there was nobody there to help them from the national body.

Competing no longer seemed important. These athletes had nobody else to turn to within British Athletics at a management level. They desperately needed someone to support them, but they were left without a psychological safety net. I found myself reverting into a leadership role that I didn't want to take up, but I was left with no choice due to the absence of alternatives from the authorities.

Collectively, we were dealing with the traumatising experiences that we had dealt with since birth. I felt that I couldn't trust anyone anymore, everything was heightened.

You started to question people's motives. I would see white former teammates post stuff in support of Black Lives Matter, and I wondered where had you been when we needed you to stand up for us? Were they just protesting to signal their virtue now that the coast was truly clear and this outcry was finally palatable for the broader public?

I never told anyone in British Athletics about the numerous incidents of racism that I had experienced while representing my country. I also never told anyone about the sexual assaults that I endured while competing under the British Athletics banner. I have spent many nights wondering if I should have spoken out, and why could I not? The answer is that I never felt comfortable that there was someone like me in the organisation who would understand what I had gone through.

Throughout my career, the vast majority of the support staff in British Athletics were white and that was the status quo. The reality is that none of them had experienced the racial discrimination that is a day-to-day event for every black athlete in the system, from childhood until the day they die.

They didn't understand the realities of black females being sexualised from a young age against their will, and the fear of judgement and shame about their bodies. I simply didn't feel safe to speak out.

Paula Dunn was a true friend and support to me, but Paula was shouldering the vast demands of this unpaid and largely unrecognised role, while being under the same pressure and demands as any head coach. It wasn't fair. She still needed to work out the strategy that was going to drive the best medal count possible. Paula remained the only black person in a leadership role in British Athletics until my close friend and former sprinter Christian Malcolm was appointed head coach in September 2020.

In the 2016 Olympics I competed in, nearly half of the athletes competing for Great Britain were black. There were 44 members of the support staff, with only 11 coming from a BAME background.

Conversely, when I started my career, I looked at my competitors from the USA and I saw their team rooms headed by an inspiring black president, Stephanie Hightower. I idolised that woman, simply because she showed me what was possible, just by looking at her. She was the boss, and she was black. Their support staff was filled with black psychologists, therapists and sports scientists. USA Track and Field didn't just talk about diversity through glossy brochures, they lived it.

I heard people question why British athletes were traumatised by what was perceived, initially at least, as an American issue, centred on the murder of George Floyd. In Britain, we can caricature the United States of America as a country that elected Donald Trump and is dealing with the legacy of Jim Crow laws that enshrined racial segregation for generations.

We look smugly at their failings and tell ourselves that in

Britain we don't have the same racial problems. The issue is, we do, it is just hidden more subtly, but I can assure you that it stings just as hard for black people across this country.

In Britain, there have been well known vicious racist murders. In 1993, an aspiring young architect, Stephen Lawrence, was murdered by a gang of white youths, with only two people finally being convicted of murder in 2012.

I was a teenager when my Dad made me read Sir William Macpherson's report on the case, which ran to 350 pages. The report found that the police's investigation into Stephen's murder was *"marred by a combination of professional incompetence, institutional racism and a failure of leadership."*

This was the Britain I grew up in, where fearing the police wasn't paranoia, it was a prerequisite for survival. This was the Britain where I saw my Dad removed from his car and questioned aggressively by the police for no reason other than the colour of his skin. His advice to me when dealing with the police was simple, *comply*. To do otherwise risked the unspeakable.

In 2005, when young Anthony Walker was brutally murdered with an ice axe in Liverpool, I understood the terror that he had felt in his last moments. The racial taunts that he had experienced that night from his murderer that he had ignored, were the same words he had heard spat at him every day at school. He was treated like an animal and killed without mercy. Chased through the streets, while trying valiantly to protect his girlfriend.

Healing

These murders scar my brain, with the raw feelings for two young men that were lost to this world for no reason beyond the colour of their skin. I walked the same streets where those young men were murdered in cold blood.

They could have easily been my brothers. These murders are splashed on the front pages of tabloids and drive almost collective indignation, then they are quickly forgotten by the media, and we ignore the subtle, everyday acts of racism in Britain, that act slowly as building blocks to foster seething hatred and ignorance.

On the track I ran with freedom, but off it, like so many of my black friends, we learned to blend into the background and tiptoe carefully for fear of arousing fear, suspicion, or worse, hatred.

When I walk into a room, particularly when I wear my hair in an afro puff, I can immediately tell when people meet me, whether they are at ease, or more often than not, intimidated. Equally, when I wear my hair straight, I almost always receive compliments and see people relax considerably when they meet me. I don't feel comfortable wearing my hair the way I want, instead, I am pressured to conform to what makes other people comfortable in this country, and also around the world.

When I was competing all over the world, I quickly got used to people touching my hair without permission, not children, but most often adults. It was particularly bad in China, Japan and Eastern Europe. You do not want to be rude, but equally, you do not want to be a novelty object. When your hair is touched like this, you are not someone with a strong intellect and a talent, you are just something to be petted.

My parents always taught me to look forwards, not backwards, often echoing the famous words of the first Ghanaian President Kwame Nkrumah, "Forwards ever, backwards never." They rarely if ever told me about individual acts of racism they had experienced when they arrived from Nigeria. This didn't mean they didn't suffer from racism, far from it. They arrived in a city where they had to scramble to find a doctor who would treat black patients. They simply refused to let racist incidents take away the love they had for their adopted land. I honestly wish I could share their equanimity.

I sat in the Royal Hospital in Liverpool at 17, receiving treatment for food poisoning. By sheer chance, I was in a cubicle next to where my mother was working another late shift as a nurse.

Mum was calmly trying to treat a drunk patient whose face was covered with blood. I was weak and barely able to move on the trolley bed, but could clearly make out the patient's slurred speech. *"Get this fucking women away from me. I'm not having a fucking nigger treating me. Do ya hear me? Get her the fuck away from me now."*

I was weak from the food poisoning and could barely move but went into fight or flight mode and stumbled out of the bed to defend my Mum. When I stepped away from the hospital that night, I realised that this was just one night where I happened to be there. What about the hundreds of nights when I hadn't been there to defend her?

The spine of our National Health Service is made up of people like my Mum, from every corner and culture of the world. They work hard to take care of our country's sick, often for minimal pay, yet they risk unprovoked hatred for their skin colour every time they start a new shift. As a society, we have to do far better and stand up and protect the very people who look after our most vulnerable citizens.

The focus on the BLM movement has had a positive effect, in that it worked to create awareness and some long-awaited change, but it also plunged a knife into the deepest recesses of many black people's scarred psyches.

We have worked hard to keep harrowing events hidden, while we try to move forward positively in our lives. I questioned everything. Why did it take a callous murder of yet another defenceless black person to actually bring about meaningful conversations?

Throughout the increasing awareness of BLM, I questioned whether everything was becoming performative. Social media was filled with profile pictures blacked out in solidarity and status updates about the latest black author that they were reading. Premier League football teams took a collective knee to show support.

Sportswear brands had their creative teams working late

nights to create the latest and greatest inspiring television adverts championing black athletes, when I had seen first-hand how little they had done to sustain the community they purported to support.

Were we supposed to be grateful for this mass of support and awareness from many white people in BLM? It was complicated. It was positive to see that people were finally educating themselves on the difficulties that black people face on a daily basis, but I wondered, where had many of these people been when we desperately needed support, when it was not necessarily a publicly accepted or indeed a socially fashionable thing to do? Why had it taken so long to get them to care about our lives?

It is easy to march with thousands of people in London for a common cause and post a status update to the acclaim of hundreds of likes when it's finally socially acceptable to do so but it is not so easy to demand change in a boardroom for your black colleagues and demand greater representation in leadership roles when it's palpably uncomfortable.

The greatest possibility for change comes far from the large audience, it happens in the small boardrooms up and down the country, where black people are barely represented across a wide field of British industries, including sport.

I never wanted to be a leader, on the track or off it, but I do know that I want to see change, and I have no choice but to keep using my voice. The onus shouldn't solely be on me and my colleagues, as black women, to drive change. I want all people to take a step back, look at my story, and see how they can change things for the better for everyone. I want people to take that brave stance in the boardroom, in the office and in the lecture hall, and see how they can drive generational change for their black colleagues.

When I told white colleagues in athletics that I had often struggled to get the most basic administration jobs while training in London, they had uniformly failed to believe me, gaslighting my experience, until Dai Greene, the World Champion hurdler, stood up for me and told them that if I was telling them I had been discriminated against, based on my background, then that was a fact. Why had it taken a white friend to have to advocate for me, and get them to finally agree that I was right? My own lived experience wasn't trusted by these friends until a white man had verified it.

I had a good degree in economics and was an Olympian, but it didn't matter in my job search during those trying years in London. My name, Anyika Onuora, was enough to alert the recruiter that not only was I black, but I was also born to a Nigerian father. I was applying on a daily basis for the most simple office job and was constantly rejected, in many cases, within a few hours of applying.

I started conducting my own social experiment after finally reaching the end of my patience threshold with another quick email saying the position was filled.

I kept my CV exactly as it was and changed my name to something very English and nondescript, such as "Diane

Smith" or "Jennifer Johnston" and reapplied for the same job a week later.

I repeated this with other unsuccessful applications. In every single case, despite not changing a single item on my CV apart from my name, I received countless interview offers.

The racism was subtle, and no doubt completely undetected in the company, but recruiters were collectively racially profiling candidates across the city and actively discriminating against black candidates. We see how the British tabloid press has almost singularly vilified the Duchess of Sussex, Meghan Markle, for having the temerity to bring up her struggles with mental health in the face of racism.

Like a pack of wolves, they have hounded her, egged on by the rapid clicks from their readers, who sit back and read about a black woman admitting that she was driven almost to the point of suicide in this country due to her treatment at the hands of an uncontrolled and baying mob.

Seemingly minor acts of racism can seem irrelevant, but ultimately, it all contributes to oppressing black people within this country, slowly but surely.

I was trying to help a range of colleagues through their own experiences of trauma, which were sparked throughout the Black Lives Matter movement, while trying to deal with my own experiences that were rising to the surface of my brain and tormenting me while I tried to sleep. The load was becoming too heavy for me to carry alone.

Healing

At the height of the protests, journalists started to contact me, asking me to comment on my own experiences of racism. I refused, simply because I felt that I, and many of my colleagues who were dealing with our own mental lacerations, were being wheeled out by an expectant media for quick soundbites, and then left alone when we really needed our stories told after the noise had cleared. They want trauma porn.

When we have painfully raked over bitter memories for their story, they are ready to move on, but we often cannot. My life is there for everyone to see online, all you need to do is type my name on Google and you will be fed a stream of statistics.

You can find my results, year by year. An athletic curriculum vitae if you like. While the timings tell part of the story of my life, how quick or slow I was as an athlete in any given year, and what medals I won, the timeline will never tell the story beyond the athletics track, away from the stadium, when the floodlights had dimmed. The fear, the joy, the hatred and the terror.

I can look at every time in a race, and I don't necessarily think about my performance, but I think about everything that surrounded it. The beautiful places I was lucky enough to visit and friendships that I made. The terror of being sexually assaulted and the brutal acts of racism. In examining those races and the stories behind them, I understood quickly that I had a far bigger one to tell.

I spoke to *The Guardian*'s Donald McRae, and ended up talking to him for well over two hours. I told Donald about my malaria and the conversation started to act almost like therapy, slowly untangling the tight knots that had been left in my mind for far too long. I eventually hung up the phone and started crying uncontrollably. I knew there was no turning back, and I needed to tell my story.

I have absolutely no fear of anybody or anything in telling my truth.

The alternative is silence and I have done that for too many years at a great cost to myself. I want people to look at black women in this country and understand the path that they are walking every single day. At school, my history books were whitewashed with heroic tales of Britain's exploits in its Empire, but none of the rich history of African civilisation, or the contribution of the Windrush generation to modern Britain. I want to encourage people to investigate the history of black people in Britain.

It is an uncomfortable history, but one that must be taught to future generations so we can understand our present so much better. It also holds the story of hope, when we look at what has been achieved by millions of black Britons over generations.

Writing this book has been a combination of therapy and trauma. Therapy, in that I have been forced to confront issues, and talk about them in the hope that they can help others. Night after night, into the small hours, I look over emails, diaries, press clippings, phone calls and text messages to construct the narrative of this book. They all bring back memories, some good, and some bad, and many that haunt me still. I cry when I must pick over the raging sore of a memory, but I know I must keep going.

At various moments in this process, I have questioned whether I want to continue writing this book and I have felt that I have no choice but to proceed. I am not writing it for me, I am writing it for people like me. I want it to be a catalyst for change.

I was taught from a young age that I would have to work 10 times harder than my white counterparts. I look back and ask, was that fair or right? I am often told that my life has built character and the tenacity that ultimately drove me to an Olympic medal against the odds. But maybe I didn't want to have to constantly overcome adversity. Maybe I didn't want to fight 10 times harder. Maybe I just wanted a level playing field to compete on.

As a black woman in Britain, you often feel like you are visible, but also invisible, at the same time. People can obviously see you, but so often, you feel that you are not being seen, or heard, when it comes to important issues.

Issues that affect how you live your life every day. I've had so much joy in my life, but also so much sadness. In taking part of this journey in writing this book, I know that I have needed to heal, and in doing so, I hope that I can help others to do the same.

My hope is that all black people across Britain can have a voice and not be fearful of the repercussions as I once was when competing for my country.

We all need to collectively demand change for black people in Britain and understand that while the race is long, it is something that we must relentlessly pursue until we have no breath left in our lungs. The fight must never end.

I have lived a life that has been filled with challenges, but ultimately, I am filled with immense gratitude. I constantly had imposter syndrome that told me that after every medal I should have done better. I was looking ahead to the next challenge, without reflecting on the joy that I have experienced.

I am learning to correct that now.

We must learn to treat others with compassion. You often do not have a clue what someone has been through until it is too late.

It is easy to be there for someone when the light is shining on them brightly, but more challenging when they are standing in the dark alone. I enjoyed so much success in my career, but the greatest prize I have won is finally finding my inner peace.

Through my story, I have spoken my truth, and my greatest hope is that I inspire many others to do the same.